My
Cadre

A Healer's Memoir

KRISTIN HEGGE HELGESON

BALBOA
PRESS
A DIVISION OF HAY HOUSE

Balboa Press books may be ordered through booksellers or by contacting:

Balboa Press
A Division of Hay House
1663 Liberty Drive
Bloomington, IN 47403
www.balboapress.com
1 (877) 407-4847

Because of the dynamic nature of the Internet, any web addresses or links contained in this book may have changed since publication and may no longer be valid. The views expressed in this work are solely those of the author and do not necessarily reflect the views of the publisher, and the publisher hereby disclaims any responsibility for them.

The author of this book does not dispense medical advice or prescribe the use of any technique as a form of treatment for physical, emotional, or medical problems without the advice of a physician, either directly or indirectly. The intent of the author is only to offer information of a general nature to help you in your quest for emotional and spiritual well-being. In the event you use any of the information in this book for yourself, which is your constitutional right, the author and the publisher assume no responsibility for your actions.

Any people depicted in stock imagery provided by Thinkstock are models, and such images are being used for illustrative purposes only.
Certain stock imagery © Thinkstock.

Print information available on the last page.

ISBN: 978-1-5043-6303-7 (sc)
ISBN: 978-1-5043-6305-1 (hc)
ISBN: 978-1-5043-6304-4 (e)

Library of Congress Control Number: 2016912089

Balboa Press rev. date: 10/17/2016

cadre |ˈkadrē; ˈkäd-; -ˌrā|

noun

a small group of people specially trained for a particular

purpose or profession : *a small cadre of healers*

Acknowledgments

For Tom, the true writer in the family. This book would not be possible without your lifelong support. You did not stand in my way despite your unease with my choices. I am forever grateful for your stability during my spiritual wanderings and I offer gratitude for your sustained willpower and strength. Writing your name within my tattooed caduceus turned out to be just what I needed and wanted. With mended hearts and shared history, we stand poised for our next adventure.

Many thanks to Sandy Stark, poet, author, for her clarifying and editing skills.

Thank you, Erin Bosch for taking a look and offering suggestions.

A special thanks to Liz Oakes and her website Healing Crystals For You.

I extend deep gratitude to all the sweet souls, seen and unseen, who have entered my healing room over the years. You know who you are. Bless you for your courageous and daring willingness to step into the unknown. May your efforts bring you eternal joy and happiness.

Preface

Spiritual and intuitive experiences are part of our normal human development. We all have them on many levels but often are unable to recognize, articulate, or share them. Intuitive powers are gifts waiting to be opened. They complement and balance our dominating power of logic. They help to awaken our creative abilities and bring the nature of the divine into human existence. They are natural and ever present guides for developing greater trust, love, and compassion for the Self. From there they go out into the world to be used for greater good and for meeting the needs of humanity. It is your right and your gift to the world to be present in this way. If you do not yet know how to do this, then it is time to begin.

This story describes a period of time in my life when I transitioned from western medicine to holistic medicine by way of opening my own holistic nursing practice. It was a time in my life that was absolutely extraordinary, occasionally lonely, and sometimes confusing. As I explored the deeper realms of my meditation, pranayama and yoga practices, more of my divine core was revealed, allowing me an inward journey that is not often discussed and is difficult to express in words. From my physical body I journeyed to the innermost aspects of my being and upon the discovery of my subtle energy body, "My Cadre," a group of unseen Spiritual Helpers, sprang to life. This revelation required me to continually step out of my comfort zone and embrace new ideas that kept me in harmony with this new reality. I consequently adopted a completely unconventional and creative style of healing that was reflected from this vantage point and I carried that style into my healing room. From this distance, I am able to look back and acknowledge what was taking place and explain it to myself and perhaps to you. In that way it has been a burden lifted and an expression of my truth. I hope you will keep an open mind as you read these words because all of these experiences are absolutely true. While you are reading this book, I am intending for you to receive a radiant healing that is perfectly suited for you at this time in your evolution, especially during the described meditations. May it be so.

The Master has no mind of her own.

She works with the mind of the people.

She is good to people who are good.

She is also good to people who aren't good.

This is true goodness.

The Master's mind is like space.

People don't understand her.

They look to her and wait.

She treats them like her only children.

Lao Tze

Introduction

"The path is exceedingly vast. From ancient times to the present day, even the greatest sages were unable to perceive and comprehend the entire truth; the explanation and teachings of the masters and saints express only part of the whole. It is not possible for anyone to speak of such things in their entirety. Just head for the light and heat, and learn from the gods, and through the virtue of devoted practice of the Art of Peace, become one with the divine." Morihei Ueshiba

I opened my holistic healing practice in the late 1990's. I thought I was well prepared for the experience. Academically, I had become nationally certified in holistic nursing, had a national certification as a nurse practitioner in women's health, and was trained in a wide array of holistic healing modalities. I recently had returned from India, where I learned ancient healing techniques not commonly known in the West. I kept up a rigorous, daily practice of yoga and meditation. This seemed a fine blend of East meets West and I felt satisfied that I was well equipped to sustain the rigors of standard nursing care in the holistic arena.

Yet soon after opening my private practice, mystical experiences started happening in my office space and to me personally, which were not part of my learning history. I had no context for these experiences and was caught completely off guard. In hindsight, I know these occurrences were destined to happen and I now appreciate the wisdom and reason for the element of surprise. Had I known before I started the business that I would be working with "My Cadre," a dimension of Invisible Healers now known to me as Guides, Masters, Angels, Helpers and all around Luminescent Beings of Light, I may have felt more prepared when they appeared. I hadn't known they even existed, not to mention the level of responsibility I assumed when I discovered this gift awaited me. Thankfully, over time I have been blessed with learning how to work side by side with these incredible Spiritual Entities who bring such joy, compassion, and great gifts to our world of human existence. And I have come to believe in a world that is invisible to most humans. Within it is mastery beyond our wildest dreams.

Part I

Chapter 1

"Nothing happens unless first a dream." Carl Sandburg

I have been in nursing one way or another since the age of 18. First as a nursing assistant, after that a registered nurse, and eventually a nurse practitioner. Like many others in the medical profession, my career was continually changing and evolving. I've always loved nursing and for a long time had dreamed about opening my own private nursing practice. Then, during my last years in traditional nursing, I really began to feel limited in what I could medically offer my patients. I was noticing increased discomfort about prescribing medications that I had little control over and that could have potential long term side effects for them. I had experienced deep healing from my own yoga practices and wanted more time to teach patients complementary methods of care for healing their bodies. I gradually had become more interested and involved in educating them about their health and the nature of disease, and less interested in delivering the medical model as expressed in traditional medicine. This inner conflict began to cause me a great deal of stress in my role as a nurse practitioner, and even though I was working with lovely colleagues who were so very understanding of my needs, it was evident I had to make a change. My approach to resolving this dilemma was to consider opening a holistic nursing practice. It soon became clear this was the path I was to follow. Momentum for change began in earnest on my 48th birthday and that's where this story begins.

I had a deep yoga and meditation practice at that time so this day began like all other days, with yoga and meditation. During the meditation I received a mental vision. Visions were not common for me then, but it was, and remains to this day, a powerful and memorable experience. In this vision, my deceased paternal grandmother appeared in my mind as though on a television screen and spoke to me. She said, "You need the rock from the house. Call your Dad." For over 30 years I had not given one thought to the rock which sat in the sunny foyer of my grandmother's house. It was a huge crystal, actually, and had apparently been brought home in the 1950's from a cave in Kentucky. No one ever called it a crystal back then. It was simply Grandma's rock.

My cousins and I chiseled off pieces of that rock for years to carry in our pockets. I have wonderful memories of sitting next to this crystal as a kid, watching the colorful light rays reflecting off the walls as the sun shone on the clear quartz crystal.

After the meditation, I decided to act on this vision, because this was a very unusual experience for me and came through as such a strong message. So I called my father. I asked him if the rock was still in Grandma's house. My bachelor uncle lived there at the time. I did not tell my dad about the vision nor did I say why I was interested in the rock. I did not know at the time why I needed it, but I felt compelled to follow through with the instructions from the meditation. My dad asked no questions, thank goodness. He simply said, "I will find out." Later that day he called to say he had the 40 pound rock in the back seat of his car and wondered what he should do with it. I told him to hold on to it for now and I would drive up to retrieve it as soon as my work schedule allowed. It turns out he dropped his plans for the morning and drove an hour to my home town, walked into my grandmother's house, and announced to my uncle that he was taking the rock. That was the end of it. Some things are just meant to be. A few days later I made the 3 hour trip to pick up the crystal.

Once it was in my home, I proceeded to clean it up and tried to figure out what to do with it. It stunk to high heaven of cigarette smoke. It was heavy! And sharp! I had to wrap a huge towel around it just so I wouldn't lacerate myself while lifting it. I set it on a cart with wheels, which made it a lot easier to maneuver. First it went into the bathtub to soak in soap and water. It was still repulsively stinky. My next idea was to bury it in the ground for a time, but it was still winter and that was impossible. So I set it inside a large cooler, filled the cooler with sand and water, and closed the lid. A few weeks later I opened the cooler, dug out the sand around the crystal, and with the help of my husband we lifted it back unto the cart. It was March by then, and we were having a spring thunder storm so I wheeled her outside to be with Mother Nature. That did it. The crystal, whom I now referred to as a "she", was dazzling and all charged up from the lightning. One thing I learned from this experience was that crystals absorb the energy of their environment. I wondered what family stories I might hear if this crystal could speak to me. I have to admit I was feeling sorry that this beauty had been so misunderstood in our ignorance over the years. But nevertheless, here she was in her pure form, sparkling like the magnificent jewel she is.

I sensed the crystal would be an integral part of my holistic healing work, but I felt clueless about how to work with her. I went to the computer and did a search on crystals. This was near the beginning of the computer era when you could actually get information from someone without buying it. The name of a woman came up who seemed to know a lot about crystals, and so I wrote her an inquiring email regarding my situation. The next day I had a response. This is what she wrote back to me:

"Dear Kris,

God Bless your grandmother. She sounds like a very special soul.

Do not ever doubt the powers inherent within yourself. You are doing some very special work - the Universe is very thankful for the path that you have chosen to follow. As far as the crystal? I'm not sure if you had intentions of using this crystal for your own personal use but this is the information that I received pertaining to your crystal. I tuned into Spirit for information in regard to the purpose of this crystal. This is what I received:

There are many Healing Masters on the other planes of existence that have been following this crystal for a long time. They knew that it would find its way to you and that the both of you would work together toward a unified goal.

It is suggested for the crystal to be placed in a water fountain in your office or foyer/entry room/reception room. The crystal is to be positioned with the termination aiming toward the entry way of the room. The crystal is to be positioned in the fountain at an angle so that the largest face on the termination is parallel with the ceiling of the room. (I am sending an image of a crystal positioned in this fashion, so that you can get the idea of what I am trying to describe).

The Healing Masters are intending to use the crystal as a medium to send focused healing energies toward the person entering the room. The person will receive a multi-dimensional healing just by walking into the room. Of course, everyone that enters the room will have given consent on a higher level for this healing to take place.

Now, as far as the benefits that you will receive in all of this? Every time you walk in front of the crystal, information will be relayed to you pertaining to the situation at hand with each client that you address. You will, in consort with the client, be working on the 3rd and 4th dimensional level, to facilitate the healing process.

Much love being sent your way, Kris. May this information be helpful to you."

Hmmm. While the letter was interesting, due to my inexperience I was not able to understand any of it. My logical mind was having a field day. Healing Masters? Other planes of existence? Unified goal? Work together? What "work" was she referring to? Multilevel dimensional healing? Parallel termination? Oh lord. It all seemed too weird.

After mulling things over for a few days, I made a decision to move forward. I could do the practical thing, which was to build a fountain for the crystal and place her in water. That much I could do. As far as the possibility of having some hidden information about people? No way. At the time it was not in my realm of conscious ability or desire, so I left it at that. Take what you can and leave the rest, as they say. Little did I know my work with the Healing Masters was about to begin in earnest. Meanwhile, I carried on as usual with my professional life but I could feel my role as a nurse practitioner at the University slipping away.

The influence of my recent yoga and meditation practices, and of course now the crystal and her intriguing story, had led to irreconcilable feelings of discontent with my University job. Holistic Medicine had not yet been organized at the University, so there was little opportunity to transfer to a more suitable environment. Western medicine places specific standards of practice on nurses, which I absolutely honor and respect. But I no longer resonated with, or desired to be a part of, that established system. I needed more independence to teach the modalities of healing that I had come to believe in.

Nursing had been the stable force in my life for 30 years and my decision to leave traditional medicine was a most difficult one. In spite of this professional history, the urge to move forward felt irrepressible. All I had to do was root out the courage to say "yes." At the time of my resignation, I felt if I was not able to find the freedom to express my soul's longing, a part of me would inevitably perish. Yet if there is a purgatory on earth it must be that agonizing space lying between the known and the unknown. Letting go of what I knew in my traditional nurse practitioner role caused a great deal of emotional strain for me. I did not know what was ahead. I was also a people pleaser and going against the grain of what other people thought I should do caused me endless grief. I worried about how they would judge me for giving up the stability and security of a good job in the state system. I judged myself for that as well. They had a point, and logically it made sense. But logic is no match for the soul, who was now trying to make her point. Until you have turned and faced your soul you cannot know its magnetic power. The financial loss would cause a hardship, but I could see it would be far more stressful if I could not honor the emerging part of me that now needed expression. I actually imagined I would have to medicate myself to quell the misery if I denied what was wanting to be birthed within me, and wondered if this is one reason women suffer from depression. I have my husband to thank for not standing in my way. He's been more than generous to me. Perhaps it would have been

8

kind to release him from our marriage when I took that fork in the road. But that's not how things turned out. We ended up going down that road together. The most difficult lesson I learned in the process of resigning was to trust myself. Spirit knocked on the door, I opened it, and walked through. There was no going back. Against all outside advice, I followed my heart and stepped away from traditional medicine.

Resigning from my University job brought back the memory of an experience I'd had with my friend, Pat, a few years prior to this time. On a lark one evening we went to a palm reading class offered by a professor at a local college. During the class the professor read our palms. She looked at my right hand and pointed to a specific descending crease extending from my lifeline, and said I would be taking a divergent path later in my professional life to help people in a new way. It was the kind of thing I didn't take seriously at the time, but I can't tell you how often I've looked at my palm since then as though it were the North Star leading to my destiny. It goes to show how we are sometimes lead to an event that will influence us in ways we cannot know about until it is presented to us in the future.

Chapter 2

"The best and most beautiful things in the world cannot be seen or even touched. They must be felt with the heart." Helen Keller

Now that I was finally able to let go and had resigned from my job the details of opening a business had to happen. There needed to be office space for the holistic work to be done. During the last week of my University employment I finally found an office in downtown Madison that seemed like a good fit. Thank you, Joan and Mare, for waiting for me that day when I was late for our appointment. Had you not been willing to wait heaven only knows where I might have landed.

Within a month I was up and running. I created business cards, wrote a nice introductory note about myself to hand out to my patients, now referred to as "clients" since they would likely pay a fee for a visit, and had an office phone number for making appointments. My crystal was placed in the fountain in my healing space. Everything seemed ready. The first few people trickled in. I did what I had learned to do: Reiki, Healing Touch, Pranic Healing, and taught others the self healing techniques of meditation, breath work and yoga. After 30 years of traditional nursing it was fun and exciting to be working with people in this new way. I could see definite changes in them and felt pleased with the work. I could also see how nursing had prepared me for the role I was to play in this new endeavor.

However, soon after opening my healing practice curious and unexplainable "events" began to happen. On an internal level, I must have been ready for them because I was able to navigate through them with surprising ease. But I was not expecting or anticipating them. They were experiences that were not measurable or quantifiable, often intangible, and therefore challenged my logical, medically trained mind. My objective mind did not know what to do with this information. I could not easily explain what was happening. I could only be a witness. My inner dialogue and journaling had given me a preview of events to come, which included a vague idea about receiving additional support if I chose to open my healing room. But I had not taken seriously or believed the information that had come through.

The first mystifying occurrence happened one evening while I was visiting my mother. We were in her kitchen fixing dinner when we suddenly noticed a "fragrance." It was the most beautiful thing I had ever smelled in my life. It was an intoxicating, wonderful, fresh, delicate scent. I asked her what perfume she was wearing. "I am not wearing any perfume. I was about to ask you the same thing", she replied. I informed her I also was not wearing perfume. The fragrance was so strong it radiated from our clothes, from our hair. Our arms smelled divine. We laughed. We were stumped. We stared at each other over dinner, expressing wonder and curiosity about this bewildering experience. The next morning I went into Mother's bedroom. The fragrance was strong in her room and it filled the entire house with sweetness. When she got out of bed she peeked around the corner of the kitchen and said, "The fragrance is my angel, Christina". I knew something inexplicable was happening, but my skeptical mind was reluctant to place an "angel" label on it. I didn't want to rain on her parade, so I smiled and said nothing.

Right or wrong, this silent response was the beginning of my strategic reaction to the unexplainable phenomena that expressed itself over and over in my office, which I now referred to as "the healing room." My clients would often convey their own intuitive interpretation of their experiences during a healing and I learned the importance of honoring their understanding. My mother woke up that morning *knowing* the fragrance was her sweet angel named Christina. I am not sure how that knowing came to her, but it did. It became her experience. For the rest of her life she occasionally felt the clear, healing presence of Christina and smelled the lovely waft of perfume. It brought her a great deal of comfort. Not only did we receive the blessing of the fragrance, which became a permanent part of my healing activities. We also received the perception of an angel which likewise became a permanent part of my healing activities. Spirit beautifully arranged that both phenomena would initially come through the avenue of my Earth Mother, and it is not lost on me now that this too was written in the stars.

The value of experience is that it brings a gift which influences our perception, our way of thinking. It becomes our truth. My mother was clear with her perception that the fragrance was her angel Christina, as it had been her experience. There is no arguing with experience. But at the time I did not know what to think. In hindsight, it is hard to believe the level of resistance I carried in order to appear "normal." I wanted to have a respected and professional independent nursing practice. I felt a wave of panic to think of the expectations others might have of me if they thought angels appeared in my healing room, connected to the fragrance. I worked at keeping an open mind and decided the best thing would be to simply stay neutral and observe. A good nursing strategy!

When I returned to the healing room after spending the weekend with Mother, I noticed the fragrance there as well. It was coming from the crystal in the fountain of water. It emitted the same wonderful, refreshing, amazing fragrance. Over the next weeks to months I noticed it on many of my clients, on children, on their toys and their clothes. I proceeded to read as many esoteric texts as I could find on the subject of spiritual healing and fragrance. To keep it simple and clarify for clients, I explained the fragrance as tangible evidence that Spirit is working through us, opening us to our natural flow of energy, and creating an avenue for the Divine to express Herself. It is the essence of Spiritual Light and is a very good sign that we are on the correct path. Now, however, I am much more inclined to say the fragrance came from the Masters themselves, the ones now working through the crystal as well as a manifestation of divinely expressed Universal Soul.

That same week I had a session with Olivia. She was 6 at the time, had been having nightmares and trouble sleeping. When she came to the healing room with her mother, she seemed immediately at ease and climbed up onto my lap. We sat together and she told me about her experiences at night and had some questions for me. "Do you talk to the angels in the dark"? "What do you say to the angels"? "Can you see the angels"? "What do the angels say to you"? Oh lord, was I really supposed to know something about angels? First my mother and now a child? At this point I had to wing it, no pun intended. I had never been able to see, or talk to, or hear angels (well, once as a kid and once recently during the middle of the night but I didn't take it seriously), and I was quite certain if angels did exist they were not going to be doing much talking. I never mentioned one thing about angels in any of my advertising or business cards so why was there an assumption I would know about angels? I felt worried, unprepared and, sad to say, irritated. I was a Western trained health care provider applying science based techniques to help others solve their dilemma of illness. Angels were not in the script. I felt unsure how to proceed. Fortunately I had my nursing skills to fall back on. I was able to navigate as the care giver and remained faithful to allowing the healing energy to express itself through me without controlling the outcome. That was an entirely new strategy. If I was truly going to be an instrument for healing I had to surrender to the work however it manifested itself.

My response to all of Olivia's questions was, "I'm not sure." When we started our session I had her lie down on my massage table, which I now referred to as my healing table, and covered her with a small blanket. Her mom remained seated in a nearby chair. I asked Olivia to close her eyes and rest. She seemed relaxed. As with all sessions, I stated an invocation prior to starting our healing work and Olivia and her mother did the same. After my hand had been resting lightly on Olivia's tummy for a few minutes the room filled with exquisite fragrance, the smell of roses. Her mother started to cry, and Olivia told us that her angels had come and were dropping rose petals onto her. She smiled. I continued to gently rebalance Olivia's energy as I had been taught to do for the remainder of the session. My mind was bursting with wonder, but I remained composed and reassuring, as though this was an everyday occurrence. Nursing impassivity once again rescued me. When she left the healing room about 40 minutes later, Olivia felt happy and reassured. Her mother later reported that her nightmares had vanished.

I cannot rationally explain what happened to Olivia and her mother. But they both had an experience that was real and influential and resulted in improved health. Again, I was the observer and had to stay open and detached from the results.

Over the next several weeks many new people came in for their first visit. Like those of us who go to a health care provider, they had medical problems that were being addressed in the medical community. They came to see me because they were seeking additional coping strategies and ways to support the body/mind connection as they continued on their road to good health. I had come to realize the inseparability of body and mind and I felt confident in applying the array of integrative strategies I had become certified in. It was particularly important to speak about the emotional and mental stress of illness, and teaching the simplicity of conscious breathing surfaced as a particularly efficient tool to strengthen this connection. After a session, the client was encouraged to practice a particular coping strategy at home and to then incorporate it into their life. I emphasized the point that making time for such good health practices should never be delayed or viewed as an inconvenience but as an absolute necessity for healthy living. I felt increasingly comfortable in this new role, and I had gained confidence in my hands on healing techniques of Reiki, Healing Touch and gentle massage.

So it startled me when I felt a powerful shift coming from within to suddenly lift my hands off of my client's body to work in an area inches to several feet away from their bodies. It was not a gradual shift. It happened spontaneously and without warning. One day I was working with hands on the physical body and later that day I was working with hands off the physical body. That style of healing has become second nature to me now, but at the time it felt like some inner wisdom had taken charge and started doing a tango in the middle of my waltz. I did not know the steps to the dance, so I had to be shown. Imagine being blindfolded while your guide dog leads you along a winding path. There is no rush as you carefully proceed, but you are cautious and alert to potential obstacles and perils along the way. My healing room experience was similar in that I was guided into a zone that was not accessible with my physical eyes. It was as though a divine Geppetto had interceded on my behalf and taken control of little Pinocchio's hands to gently guide them with invisible, celestial strings. I felt my hands rising up and off of my clients physical body to rest in an area about a foot away from them. At that point I was coached to intuitively use my breath as a stabilizing influence. With the application of the breath, it felt as though a supernal tuning fork had emerged from within me to stabilize the energy field and vibrationally perfect a unified chord of equilibrium for the client. Perfect balance was achieved in this unseen space. Unbeknownst to me, my pranayama skills had been growing stronger as a result of my personal meditative practices. I had not anticipated the use of breath in this way as a method of healing. When it happened on that day, I struggled to maintain my inner composure with my clients but proceeded as though this were the most natural thing in the world.

The wise will tell you it takes time to learn a craft. We learn and then we assess, we learn some more and then re-assess. So it goes with the art of healing. In spite of my Western trained medical mind, which held great resistance to anything outside the realm of physicality, phenomena was happening that required me to suspend my judgement. First the fragrance, and then the unexpected lifting of my hands to an invisible space around my clients. I later learned to call this area the "energy body." Paranormal activities continue to happen to this day with every person who lies on the healing table and those activities are beyond understanding. In the beginning I was amazed to hear reports of people's experiences during a session. And so it seemed true, this message I received while journaling some years ago. "Open your practice and We will come." I wondered, who are the "We"? Do Guides and Yogis and Angels really play a part in our human journey? Do they work through us to help humanity? Is it really possible to have contact with Them? Was I really working with the Masters? And if so, who are those Masters? What part of my brain was involved with this work? How did I know I was on the right track?

These are the questions that brought curiosity to my doubting, resistant, and now worried mind. Even though I proceeded with great faith into my healing room, I was not certain how to answer these questions. No Spirit had ever appeared to me and said "I am real." So I had to make it up in the beginning. I had to find a way to trust the healing work that was emerging. First the faith, then the evidence. The unseen and invisible Energies working with me in the healing room were doing their best to give me proof of their existence. But I had plenty to say about it. If I'd written a note to them and left it on my healing table overnight it might have said something like this:

Dear Angels and Other Invisibles,

If you are here, let me say I must retain complete ownership of my healing room. It is my healing room, my practice, my relationship with the clients on the line. I set the tone for all energy work in my healing room and I have definite rules, the first one being that all energy work is for the highest good of the person on the table. I can and will move over to make room for you who come to bestow blessings on my clients, but all work will need to come through me to reach that person. It is my responsibility to each individual who comes for a healing to navigate this path safely on their behalf. I insist on Love as the highest principle.

Yours Truly

Chapter 3

"Start by doing the necessary, then the possible, and suddenly you are doing the impossible." St. Francis of Assisi

As was expressed in the letter about the crystal, I did seem to have some knowledge of the condition of illness that presented in people who came to the healing room. Surprisingly, it was there in a flash. And yet it seemed that I was not the one making the assessment. It was simply known. There were no words to describe that knowing. A higher source of wisdom manifested itself through me. While I was listening to the client tell about the details of their life and what brought them in to the healing room, I was made aware of an entirely different form of communication on a higher level. I seemed to be in two worlds at once. Again, my nursing experience taught me to stay calm. On this inner level there was clear understanding of the problem, as though it was all predetermined before the person arrived in the healing room. While I did take into consideration the expressed difficulty of the client, it seemed there had already been an agreement on a higher level between the one who came for a healing and whatever invisible Energy was assisting them. I intuited, or saw in my mind, this Energy as devoted Spirit Beings who were standing in the Great Light, unified, skilled, and qualified to render service, right there in the room with me. I say "Beings" because truly, I had no other word to use. They were not "people" like you and me, as they really had no form. The power of love and devotion emanating from Them was utterly remarkable. I would like to say I was invited to merge with Their realm of existence, but the truth is I was already unified, as though we were one seamless body, interconnected and inseparable. It was just a matter of altering my focus. They were available to me in an invisible and unfamiliar layer of reality that I had to slowly feel my way into. This layer of reality resided in the subtle bodies that surround the physical body where I had been guided to place my hands. I didn't yet understand that I was being invited to act as a medium to transfer energy - later known to me as "new age medicine" - between the worlds. That understanding would come much later. And I didn't know then that as my heart grew stronger, I would completely surrender to the energy of these elegant and invisible Teachers. But I did realize that I was truly in the midst of a Creative Force so much greater than my half-pint self, and that the people coming into the healing room were likely involved in an evolutionary contract of some kind with an evolving nature far more expansive and advanced than what I could even imagine. I wish I could say I completely trusted the Energy, because I really wanted to. But I was wary, and looking to find sure footedness with regards to where my clients and I were headed. Fortunately, Spirit came to my rescue and sent me my second vision.

I had to make a decision regarding how to proceed. I was prepared for doing certain afore mentioned healing techniques which I had diligently practiced. While these techniques were useful, it seemed something entirely new was emerging. I was being invited to work in consort with Energies on a higher level who had all but taken over my healing room. These Energies reflected the true identity of divine perfection for those clients entering the healing room. Their exquisite nature cannot be put into words. In hindsight I can see that this too was prearranged, but I had not seen it coming.

Since I had such a huge measure of doubt and was not yet used to the presence of these Spirit Energies, I worried about working correctly and safely. Consequently, I invoked all the holy names I could think of before a healing session to assert my authority in the healing room. I wanted to cast a wide and inclusive net so I enlisted the help of Jesus, Buddha, Allah, Shiva, Mother Mary, Archangel Michael, the Yogi's, the Masters and many other great saints of the Universe. I also searched for and found my son's ninja sword just for good measure. I wanted as much protection as possible, not only for myself but for everyone who came to the healing room. I vowed to use the power of that sword on any energy not for the highest good and in alignment with my spoken words and invocations. The sword became a symbol of strength and security for me, and I felt reassured to have it lying under the healing table. From time to time I would nick my toe on it, so I can tell you from experience the sword energy was potent.

At the end of a particularly busy day I sat alone in the healing room, considering the situation. I was experiencing a great deal of angst. Could I really trust the Energies working with me? Was I capable of doing this new healing work that I suddenly felt so unprepared to do? What was happening in this healing room that seemed so far beyond my understanding? What was my role with the "Invisibles"? I was worried in general, but especially because I thought I needed to pick one deity to rely on. It was all so confusing. When I looked up, I saw the vision. In the vision, there was a semi circle of beautiful figures. They were holding hands. Sweetness filled their benevolent faces. They were all races, genders, religions. Each one represented a particular teaching. A ribbon connected Their hands and from this semi- circle of figures the ribbon wound its way upward to one umbrella. I knew at that moment that my angst was over when I realized all religions and teachers were under the same umbrella. I did not have to choose - it was all under one guardianship. Whew. It was incredible to be in the midst of this knowing.

And so I began to lean into these formless Energies which came to be of service. Another open door to walk through. Little by little, I practiced being in Their company, allowing Their energy to be part of the healing circle. I concentrated on listening with one ear to the person on the healing table while also paying attention to the delicate, intricate interchange of energy on higher levels between that person and the Invisible Ones who were present to work with them. My ability to be in two worlds at once was surprising, but that aspect of the work was beginning to feel more familiar and less daunting. It was feeling more natural to anchor energy exchange in this way. For example, while the client was talking about a specific problem on a physical level, the Helpers were already several steps ahead assisting energetically, or spiritually, with resolution of that very problem in the client's "energy body" where emotions and thoughts resided. I felt reassured by the memory of a recent prophecy told to me by my friend, Rainbow Hawk, after I shared with him an amazing experience I had while fishing with my brother.

My brother, a consummate fisherman and story teller, and I had gone to the lake on a beautiful, warm summer day. We were on the water in the paddle boat, meandering, talking, and relaxing. He had two fishing poles in the water. Casting out, reeling back, casting out, reeling back. We heard a squawking racket and turned to see a few crows circling an eagle who was sitting in a tree on shore. My brother looked away to the North, and continued fishing as he told me this story: "One day while fishing on North Lake I saw an eagle sitting peacefully in a tree. Suddenly a bunch of noisy crows started circling the eagle, badgering and attacking it. After a few minutes the eagle lifted up its talon, took a swipe at the crow, and ripped out its stomach." As my brother was telling me this story, I continued to watch the eagle on the shore. I saw it sitting peacefully in the tree. I saw the crows circling it, then begin to badger and attack the eagle. Then I watched the eagle lift its talon to swipe at the crow's belly just as my brother was saying those exact words. I am used to having magic happen when I am with my brother, as he is quite the sage, but this was jaw-dropping. The eagle then sprang from the pine tree branch and swooped over us, dropping a feather some yards from our boat. We paddled over to the gently floating feather where my brother cast his fishing line. He pulled out a big bass. This all happened within 5 incredible minutes. A few weeks later I related this story to Rainbow Hawk, who gifted me with an interpretation that resonated. "One who has such an experience would have the ability to witness simultaneous stories in more than one world." The experience is also a reminder of the power of the spoken word and how our words reflect and influence our reality.

The memory of this story helped me to stay centered and focused while adjusting to the new energy of the healing room. In this fishing story, experience came to be my teacher. Since that time I have stayed mindful to observe what is happening in the physical world while doing deep healing work with an individual. Sometimes when we remove unwanted patterns of energy in a person who has come to the healing room, they will say it feels like a weight has been lifted. Then a garbage truck will suddenly drive by. Or a jack hammer will be heard outside the window when we are penetrating the consciousness of old habits and thought forms that are hard for an individual to release. The physical world will reflect and offer insight to affirm inner changes so that we can better observe and understand them. It is not so much magical as it is practical.

And logical. Spirit sends synchronicity as a means to unify and anchor our perceptions.

If you keep looking you will find these affirmations all around you.

Chapter 4

"Because one believes in oneself, one doesn't try to convince others. Because one is content with oneself, one doesn't need other's approval. Because one accepts oneself, the whole world accepts him or her." Lao Tze

Now that I was feeling more comfortable with the Spirit Beings involved in the healing work, I knew I had to re-evaluate my intentions and also change the language used to describe my holistic services. I was transitioning from a very traditional, documentation-oriented system of medicine into a world of mystery, where language was secondary to experience. Nurses are used to documenting the progress of patients, which is standard procedure in any medical practice. However, it was difficult to translate the healing experience into words. There was no protocol to describe what was happening in my healing room. I tried in the beginning, and could couch the mystery behind a teaching concept. For example, "Tia was seen today for the complaint of anxiety. She regularly visits her health practitioner, and is requesting additional guidance from a holistic perspective. Diaphragm breathing exercises were explained and demonstrated with specific emphasis on tension release around the belly." This kind of superficial documentation was perfectly fine and was acceptable language to satisfy the legal requirements for a nursing practice. However, it was incomplete and frankly dishonest. There was no mention of the exchange of energy between Tia and her Invisible Healers and yes, likely Angels, who gathered around the table and attended to the deeper levels of her being. It felt dishonest to pretend these Attendants didn't exist, but I was afraid to write the truth. "Invisible healers highlighted Tia's right kidney, released negative substance, exquisitely balanced and harmonized the second chakra, radiated light, blessing infused, balanced and affirmed." Oh my. How would I defend myself against the ridicule when I became tongue tied before the board of nursing who would no doubt call me in and confiscate my nursing license? My imagination ran wild with potential scenarios. Better to keep my head down and not mention the orchestrations of our healing. Our healing sessions were about evolutionary process, consciousness, and something way beyond nursing protocol. I had placed a high expectation on myself to come up with a rational explanation to tell others what was happening in my healing room and to this day I fall short of that ideal.

It took a while to ease into knowing that my job was simply to be a coach, to help birth new energy, and allow for nature to gently take its course. Once again, due to the element of surprise, I had not prepared myself for the documentation dilemma. Eventually I found I had less and less tolerance and ability for developing documentation strategies. Today I would be much more capable of handling the issue. Blessings to all who have since stepped out in this world of holistic medicine and are able to blend the documentation process with the spiritual process. I honor you. At the time, I was focusing all my concentration on learning how to collaborate with the Invisibles. So to make things easier, I made the decision to drop most of my hard earned credentials.

Dropping my credentials brought incredible freedom and also loss. And some years later, perhaps regret. But until I was truly able to let go of who I was and trade her in for who I was becoming, I was limiting myself. Having to play by someone else's rules had become impossible. I wanted complete freedom to explore the world presented to me as a healer without the hindrance of administration and board regulations. Certainly there was a lot of apprehension in making that decision. I had to remind myself that I retained the experience of all my years of nursing and was now simply stepping into another realm of learning. I felt free to reinvent the language needed to bring more authenticity to my healing practice. I also felt free to talk with clients about my perceptions of what was happening during healing sessions. I could be more truthful. This meant I would actually have to trust what I was intuiting. Did I dare take the risk? It felt a little bit like quicksand. The old giving way to the new. I felt the need to have a new statement to explain myself to folks who came in for a healing. There were so many questions from others. I did not know where to start. Frustration led to a meditation which had become a very useful transformation tool for me. You know how it is sometimes when you have to take your little self aside and quietly listen while your bigger Self gives you a pep talk? Here is what I wrote after the meditation:

> *Energy practice. Using energy in new ways to heal others and yourself. It is all about energy. Energy in thought forms, psychic healing beyond the realm of traditional, typical nursing as you know it. It is nursing in a new way. Your nursing skills are very much needed and used. You cannot separate who you are from what you do. You have simply taken your craft to a new level where Universal Energies, truths, and concepts are used in a new way. You are not yet used to it, but in time it will become very familiar to you. Right now you may feel a bit*

out of your element, but be assured that you are very capable. Perhaps you could rearrange your brochure to articulate what has happened and that you offer new age medicine where the primal source of healing becomes the combination of a patient's consciousness and the Universal Energy embodied within that person. It does not have to be stressful. You are offering a new concept in the realm of healing. Make it an offering. A service where others can come and experience, "try on" some new ideas, new concepts, and ways of imagining. This does not have to contradict your past nursing experience. Make it fun. Be who you are and not what others think you should be.

I wondered what part of my brain was saying these things to me. But there you are, intuitive nature. After the meditation I wrote my new brochure.

The Healing Room

This holistic healing practice is dedicated to supporting and encouraging spiritual, emotional, mental, and physical growth. It is a service offered for the purpose of trying on new ideas, concepts, and ways of imagining. Each session is experiential. The modalities offered are based on energy practices, ancient healing techniques, and new age medicine, where the primal source of healing becomes the combination of one's consciousness and the Universal Energy attached to that consciousness. Sessions are unique and original, based on the spiritual requirements specific to the moment. Beings of Light - Angels, Guides, Masters, Spiritual Teachers and invisible Helpers - are welcomed and present at every healing. One may not always be aware of their presence, which is normal.

Rewriting my brochure brought more freedom to chart a new course for myself while exploring the deeper, intuitive nature of the work I was involved in. It also created greater capacity to examine the nature of the Helpers who came to work in companionship with the clients who entered the healing room. I was beginning to feel more comfortable working in two worlds at once, concentrating on listening and speaking to the client while being available to those invisible Helpers who brought New Medicine - or perhaps it was actually Old and Sacred Medicine - from the worlds beyond.

While each healing was specific to the needs of the client, similar repetitive patterns were emerging. We worked on the same glands, the pineal and pituitary, the same areas of the body, the energy centers known as the chakras, and over time it became clear that we were involved in creating a very unique style of healing. I say we because I now understood I was not working alone - it was always a group effort between the client, myself and the Attending Helpers. The Helpers would reflect a gift in the form of Light for me to radiate to the client on the table. I had the sense that on inner levels, this Light was rebalancing and strengthening fundamental coping skills for the client so they would be better equipped to handle changes that were happening on a personal and planetary level. We were "replacing" the old with the new, much like upgrading a computer. We were also helping them to become more connected to their spiritual, intuitive nature via the chakra system. I was astounded to see how integral this system was to Divine Awareness. Believe me, no one was more surprised than me to be in the midst of this exchange. I had no words for the gifts that came from these magnificent Beings of Light, so I kept silent and quietly did the work. I began to refer to these gifts simply as "medicine." Often they seemed to be qualities of peace, freedom, wisdom, love, expansion, clarity, affirmation or well being. Whatever was needed by the consciousness of the individual on the table came through the veil as specific medicine for that individual. Always the quality came to balance and harmonize a particular energy center. Sometimes the medicine acted like a solvent, so an old, worn out pattern could be released. It was important to tell the person on the table the medicine was coming so they could experience it. If the client was able to articulate, they would say the medicine looked like a color, or a shape, a light, or perhaps a word. Sometimes they would feel an emotion. As the mediator, I would be asked to receive the medicine from the Helper, hold it long enough for it to become vibrationally stable in this dimension, then carefully pass it on to the one on the healing table. This is how we co-created.

I felt the level of compassion from the delivering Helpers, and that is how I learned to recognize Them individually. Personally I did not have to know what was needed, but I did have to insist that my clients receive exactly what was required by them at that time in their evolution for their greatest good and the greatest good of all concerned. I had to learn to implicitly trust, with all my heart, the Energies I turned to who came to the healing room to assist with the healing and truly believe, without a shred of doubt, that we could proceed into this exchange of energy safely and with the purest intentions. This is the leap of faith so many healers have learned to take. It is not easy. But without it, we cannot expand into the freedom of becoming an open door for the passage of the Light.

In the healing room, I was witnessing so much beyond my human comprehension. Had there been anything in my life so far to prepare me for this? I needed to find a reasonable context for these experiences, based on my perceptions. This was not just another day in the office - or hospital - or clinic. How could I ever explain to my clients what was really happening on the healing table? I needed to tell a story that could normalize the paranormal. If people had not returned to the healing room saying they felt a shift for the good, I would have been discouraged. But to my great surprise, folks started to notice improvement, and word of mouth brought more and more people to the healing room. So we kept at it. The conclusion I eventually put to words was the best I could do to attempt a description of the interactions within the healing room. Here it is:

There is medicine in the Invisible World from ancient pools of wisdom. The medicine is brought forth by the Wisdom Keepers who have access to deeper knowledge and hold the vision for our collective, evolving species. They are present in this healing room and will remain present at every healing. Think of the medicine as a blessing, a gift that holds great Light. Soul is the divine inspector of this blessing and acts on your behalf. The medicine is gently brought into your energy centers where it creates greater union within your Self. We sometimes refer to these energy centers as your chakras. They are points of entry for this medicine. Spirit is connected to the body through this chakra system. The medicine placed in your chakra system is alive with consciousness and creative potential. It helps awaken dormant areas within you and exposes that part of your true nature most needed in the world today. It has magnetic resonance, which helps your organs assimilate new information within your body's energy system. It ultimately helps you to remember who you are. To have awareness of this energy is indeed Divine.

This conclusion inspired me to create what I would forevermore call my "Council of Ancient Wisdom Keepers." I chose the names from the sacred texts I was reading at the time. I imagined an Etheric Council, a body of assigned Masters and Yogis whom I declared as my Circle of Elders/Confidants, my Holy Ones, who held vibrational stability for me. Was I even allowed to do such a thing? I visualized some sort of deft rearrangement happening in the heavens to accommodate my request. I settled on names I felt comfortable with, and my heart sings in gratitude for the understanding reflected back to me from this conceived council. I may have to answer for this if I ever get to those pearly gates, but at that moment in time I needed the support and protection of such lineage. I invoked this Council of Ancient Wisdom Keepers before every healing and relied on the great strength of those sacred names.

I was re-evaluating my role in relationship to my clients as well, and thoroughly explored ideas on what it meant to be a healer. Whatever ideals I held about myself flew out the window. Obviously, I wasn't the one doing the healing at all. It happened between the one on the healing table and the Helpers. It was essential that I refrained from determining how the healing should take place, so Divine Light could flow and set in motion what was necessary for each client. I provided the space and acted as the messenger, but otherwise the healing work itself was being done through me, not from me. Together the client, the Helpers, and myself formed a sacred triangle. This was mostly satisfying for the clients, but also confusing and of course they had endless questions. The questions themselves became a sticky wicket because - pride goeth before the fall - I wanted them to think I knew exactly what I was doing. And mostly I did, but honestly, the mystery of a healing in its entirety takes a long time to unravel. There is so much involved when considering such an outcome. Illness, whether on a mental, physical, emotional, or spiritual level, is rarely sudden and it's all connected. The body gives clues along the way. Has the client on the table been paying attention to the clues? Are they capable of recognizing them? Are there careless habits that need correction? Are they able to see their body as a precious instrument that needs to be taken care of? Do they believe they are worthy of being healed? I, also, had endless questions. Was I doing the right thing? Was I putting the client in harm's way? I was used to following in the footsteps of others, not paving my own way, particularly when it came to trusting my intuition. It was new territory. I knew I must have been well prepared on inner levels, or things never would have unfolded as they did. Surely the face of some indwelling, divine confidante lead the way, and I clung mightily to her coattails. In spite of my human trepidations however, I was developing a true feeling of compassion and total involvement with the clients. I wanted to instill confidence in their ability to bring about a healing for themselves. Genuine concern helps regenerate the healing forces in every individual. The intensity of this attitude came from the atmosphere of the Helpers. Being in Their presence lifted us all up to another plateau, and made it easier for the leftover sludge of normal existence to fall away, exposing the beauty and wonder of new possibility. We glimpsed perfection as seen through the eyes of the Helpers, and that is how They viewed each and every person who ever entered the healing room.

Chapter 5

"Do not go where the path may lead, go instead where there is no path and leave a trail." Ralph Waldo Emerson

And so I will tell you, from my limited perspective, a bit about these magnificent Spirit Beings who lovingly attended the healing sessions. There were many, many of them present at each healing, the force of Their presence varying from subtle to powerful. Usually They were very close to the physical body, often right in front of or over the body. Sometimes They were several feet away, so far away we had to wait for their arrival. Compare it to being among very old and familiar friends, or in the company of your dearest loved ones. I had specific Helpers working with me whose invisible forms were always very nearby. Their chakras - or energy centers - acted as transformational resources and allowed unbelievable exchanges between dimensional realms. I say this knowing it sounds far-fetched, but, in my case, truth is stranger than fiction. The technical term for chakra is a sanskrit word that means wheel. I often referred to them as energy centers. They are spherical energy points in the subtle body that connect us to our life force. They are close to the physical body but not a part of it. There are seven major chakras from head to knees that correlate to major organs in the physical body. They are not visible to most people. You may believe or not believe, but I'm here to tell you that the Visionary Sources of Light working in my healing room communicated their intelligent compassion and healing skills via this system.

I can also tell you that there are supreme Life Forces within your very own chakras that continually communicate through that system to realms beyond your awareness. As was evidenced to me, we are not the only creatures with a chakra system, as often during a healing I reached through the energy centers of my Helpers to retrieve a substance needed for the client on the table. It seemed clear to me the Helpers hovering in our healing circle were symbiotically and vibrationally connected to a similar energy residing within the client's chakra system, as within so without. The impression I received was that They were functioning as one team under the authority and direction of a skillful Overseer who arranged such divine interchange on behalf of the client. The only barrier to their communal exchange was the physical body. They were working together on behalf of the client, and there was no time to waste. We got right to work. Again, knowing exactly what was needed came into play. It was as though the Sacred Energies in our healing room had prepared in advance and knew all there was to know about the precious client lying on the healing table.

The actual treatment took place once the client was comfortable and relaxed. As the Energies gathered into our circle, a vibrational forcefield was established around us. We affirmed our positions, like surgeons in an operating room, and began our work together. We routinely used the techniques of magnetism and radiation. Often a healing substance was simply handed to me which was infinitely easier than using a specific acquisition technique. Then, before radiating this delicate substance into the chakra of the one receiving the healing, I rebalanced it through my own energy centers to stabilize it in our third dimensional environment. I was learning how to do this in my morning meditations. The substance, which I referred to earlier as medicine, was absorbed into the client's chakra as a portal of entry. From there it miraculously found its way to the area in need of healing. We would then rebalance that center. When one center was specifically treated we rebalanced the others in likewise fashion.

A client usually came to the healing room with a specific problem to work on. However, it was my experience that the root of this problem was often something that remained hidden and entirely different than what was manifested to them in the physical world. The incredible Helpers within the healing circle had awareness of the root of this problem, and addressed the genesis of it sometimes before the client even entered the healing room. If there was a way to communicate to the source of this disturbance, They would find a compassionate and tender way to do so. Likewise, the medicine itself was wonderfully attuned to client's needs, and consistently found its way to the hidden injury. Almost always there had been an emotional trauma somewhere in the client's past, and it remained buried deep within that aspect of the body. It was not at all unusual for the client to feel emotion while on the table as the source of the problem came into their awareness and was released. Nothing can be healed until it is faced. However, we were able to remove a certain amount of distress without the client's knowledge simply because of the existence of Love. This was the nature of the Helpers. Sometimes the softening of an attitude or recognition of a past difficulty needed to be honored and released by the client. As human beings, we easily get stuck in mental and emotional patterns that hinder our evolutionary progress towards happiness. When faced, these patterns can be skillfully removed from one's energy field by applying the right medicine. Compassion, for example, is a treatment for suffering and is medicine for the soul to use as a solvent for all sorts of deeply imbedded mental and emotional scars. However, once a scar is removed we must retrain ourselves and take caution to try to not repeat situations that caused the problem in the first place. This is where I was able to bring forth information for the client, if they were willing to change, by offering gentle suggestions on how to accomplish that.

There was no conversation between myself and the Helpers during a healing. There was no need, as action happened simultaneously with thought, telepathically faster than the blink of an eye. The spoken word was useless in Their dimensional existence, though obviously required in ours. I learned to give one word statements like "good" or "great" to affirm safe and complete transfer of energy. To humor myself, I sometimes imagined the Helpers to be as visually impaired in my dimension as I was in Theirs. Seeing only a small hand reaching up through the clouded veil, They, in turn, would then place a beautiful object in it and attentively wait for the utterance of an echoed sound after the hand disappeared. Or, They would stand by, repositioning Themselves in case that hand needed to penetrate one of Their energy centers. Who knows? Perhaps They are telling Their own story about me, a strange woman from another dimension, whose hand appeared out of nowhere to retrieve medicine and who could only be seen by Them during her meditations when higher vibrations lifted her out of her dense body and into Their heavenly existence.

During sessions, I used certain pass words, when prompted, to enter sacred chambers inside the energy centers. These words had not been rehearsed, but simply came out of my mouth on cue. I sensed there were Sentries behind locked doors deep within one's chakra system. Until the correct password was spoken, a specific door could not be opened. This illustrates the preciousness of the qualities and creative abilities lying hidden within those sacred chambers. Everyone within our healing circle took their place and knew exactly what was to be done. The Helpers were utterly respectful, shy, non-intrusive. They often had a tender playfulness. A prayer, similar to this one taken from Alice Bailey's work, *A Treatise On White Magic,* was said by me before every healing;

"With purity of motive, inspired by loving hearts, we offer ourselves for this work of healing. This offer we make as a group and to the one we seek to heal."

And my own prayer;

"This healing is for _____ for their highest good and the highest good of the Universe at this time in their evolution. We ask that their Healers and Guides be present to release that which is no longer useful and bring that which is now needed. We are surrounded, created, sustained and protected by the Divine Light we are ever moving into."

I raised my left arm as the signal, and like the conductor leading her orchestra, we began the delicate work of weaving in the new and releasing the old. A window opened, revealing another dimension that held potential for the one receiving the healing and the many Energies waiting to be of service. At this level, the exchange was between the Inner Being of the individual on the table, some might call this the Soul, and the Etheric Attendants assisting me in the healing room. An interchange happened on inner levels between the two forces, and when the correct remedy had been retrieved by the Attendants whose range was limitless, I became the medium, or point of transfer, from one dimension to another. Can you imagine how much mental effort it would have taken to try to figure out the exact details of how all of this was done? I realized early on that if I spent too much time trying to comprehend the unknown, I would completely exhaust my energy reserves. As Rumi said, "one can go blind" trying to understand the mystery. Earlier I referred to a "predetermined agreement" that seemed destined to be fulfilled. This is where that agreement emerged. It was all arranged for individuals on inner levels long before they entered the healing room.

The Angels, Masters, and other Spiritual Beings of Light also emitted unique and amazing fragrances not of this world. One cannot imagine the healing effect this had on people. Doubts disappeared. There is nothing like tangible evidence to draw people into the great mystery. We may never fully understand this mystery, but we can be in the midst of it by experiencing it through our senses. Hearing, tasting, seeing, touching, smelling. And the sixth sense, "knowing." When we know, we bypass the intellect. Many of our experiences cannot be defined logically. They are meant to help us nurture the sixth sense, and develop our intuitive nature. And once that quality is more developed, we begin to have greater trust and confidence in ourselves and our place in the world.

When the great Teachers appeared, except for the pause of a brief greeting, I kept my head involved in the work lest I be consumed by the magnetic force of indescribable love. Each Energy attending the healing contributed their own quality and strength to it. It was not my business to try to peek at another healer's abilities, nor was it the time to be spellbound by the presence of Great Light. We had a collective job to do and we carried on professionally as Healing Energies came and went, depending on the needs of the client. It was a matter of the heart. A deep sense of compassion was held in the common heart I shared with these Energies during a healing session, and to this day I spend a lot of time in gratitude that this glorious exchange was possible. The client, meanwhile, was usually unaware of the great blessings coming to them. It was typical for them to fall asleep or remain in a restful, calm state of being.

We weren't simply offering a relaxation technique to our clients, however. Whether they knew it or not, we were there to give that person what they needed. There's that contract again. The Helpers seemed evolutionary in their natures, and, may I say, determined to bring about certain restorative changes to help the clients realize their full potential as human beings. When the client was ready, we carefully retrieved what I would refer to as an embryonic "seed" of potential from the storage of a specific chakra center. It felt to me like that little seed had been waiting eons for this expressed moment in time. The seed was then affirmed and baptized into this dimension by a Loving Presence who whispered prayers and breathed life into it. Then, ever so gently, I directed the enlivened seed toward the body, where it was reabsorbed into the chakra system. Once the seeds were sown, light was radiated to the area, and a "job well done" was proclaimed. A little water, a bit of sunshine, and the seeds could sprout.

The true nature of those blessed seeds cannot be fully known. But I do believe they were supremely holy, full of enlightenment, protected and hidden away deep in sacred chambers until the time came to once again be of service. Exquisite timing on many levels brought about this opportunity to do so. The perfect qualities the seed embodied stimulated progress for the client toward greater capacity for love, understanding, and realization of their Self as I AM. Nothing was ever wasted in the healing room. I came to believe that if these seeds could not have been used to their full potential, they would never have been released. It generated great joy around the healing circle when we were able to celebrate such a birthing event. In that way I came to believe the purpose of co-creating with these beautiful Energies was to enliven the dormant aspects within my client's energy centers where life had been asleep. We were all the benefactors of those enlivening qualities that brought the capacity for momentum and evolution. Without this exchange, I began to wonder if we as a human race would be able to fully wake up. Each encounter brought my clients closer to an existing unity within themselves, as these Healers held the vision for that eventual outcome.

The utter joy of being in the presence of Angels, Masters and Beings of Great Light cannot be fully described. It has to be experienced. It changes you. It expands you. It also requires you to remain satisfied with all other aspects of life which are so radically limiting by comparison. One cannot continue in this world as the same person after being touched by the Energies from these other dimensions.

While working with Them, there was no speaking. There was only knowing. They filled my healing room with joy, compassion, wisdom, and medicine for the future. Medicine that was waiting to be absorbed into those wonderful energy centers of ours we have yet to learn so much about and which hold unlimited potential for our evolutionary progress. I came to regard the Helpers as guardians of the human race because

They seemed to know where we were headed in the unfoldment of our full potential as human beings.

Many people asked me what these Invisible Energies looked like. That is not for me to say. I prefer not to describe them for you and here's why. My physical eyes only work for me in this third dimensional reality. The Helpers are Etheric Beings, or Beings who reside in the ethers. As a tactile healer, I used my sense of touch, and though I received an impression, the Helpers generally did not take form. There are many wonderful folks, and you may be one of them, who are able to visualize Beings in higher realms and can describe them to you. We have pictures of the Angels and Masters that tell us it is so. But all information comes through an individual's mind differently, as it should be, and everyone who tries to describe them may have a contrasting description.

Although at first I tried, I later realized it was not my job to describe Them. It was my job to work with Them and help my clients open to their own intuitive nature. I completely understood my client's desire's to "see" however, and it took me a long time to let go of my own need in that regard. But I have to say that a part of me did not want to relinquish intuition to logic and I tried to encourage others to form their own impressions.

I used the sense of touch and subtle vibration during healing sessions. When my heart opened and we became One Energy working on behalf of the the person on the table, there was no separation between us and I lost all interest in describing Them. It didn't matter. Using words in that way only served to distract from the healing and brought language into an arena that was too exquisitely delicate to handle the dense vibration of words.

So you may use your imagination. I know Them through their compassionate natures. I rarely looked directly at Them. We worked in consort, side by side, with one intention - to bring healing to the one on the table. While there was certainly a palpable atmospheric lightness in Their presence, we took our work very seriously and during a session we concentrated on the work that needed to be done. There was a brief hello when a Healer entered the circle and an affirmation at the end of the healing that indicated complete balance had been achieved. We bowed, offered gratitude, and stood facing the Light of the client on the table who had received the treatment. Believe me, I had to work on the correct deportment - one of neutrality - in order to be a helper to the Helpers and allow this energy to move as it did between the worlds.

Inner sight is available to all of us. It is an indwelling ability that, when nurtured, brings greater intuitive knowing and certainty of right action. To impress upon you the enormous importance of developing the intuitive nature waiting to be born within you is the most important aspect of my writing. Matured intuition is the best way to remain comfortable in this world. It helps us connect to our spiritual nature, to know ourselves as ancient beings, and develops self confidence to navigate our human lives. When we talk about developing our intuitive nature, one might say we are actually moving, or expanding into, a greater aspect of ourselves - one that is more giving, more open, more receptive. If we continue to expand into what is possible within us in this way we develop attitudes and actions that seem beyond our capacity to mentally invent. We start to dissolve old patterns, we become more loving, we accept death more easily, we start to behave in ways that seem to be of an entirely different nature. We start to feel connected to others and realize that the impact of our actions can affect them. We start to become awakened. One begins to feel greater than human limitations. A feeling of well-being sets in. This creates a deeper sense of wonder and one can proceed into life with a broader view of possibilities. Healing can occur when we remember what we have forgotten about our connectedness, our unity and interdependence.

For myself, my intuitive nature was quite dormant until I started a particular yoga and meditation practice two and a half years before opening my holistic nursing business. You do not necessarily need a yoga practice, although it is good for you to do so for general good health, in order to develop your intuition. There are many modalities that can help you. The exercise I offer has helped many people and is derived from the tradition of Kundalini Yoga. It comes from a practice I first learned as a yoga student and also comes from my healing room, which is where I first started advising people to use this practice. I guess it would be safe to say I learned the techniques from the Helpers, as we applied them time after time during sessions with clients. There are many ways to open to Spirit - this is simply one way.

Raising Intuitive Awareness

Set aside 15 minutes to do this exercise. Lie down, one hand on your belly, the other hand resting at your side. Inhale. Be sure your belly rises as you inhale. If you are inhaling with your chest, practice changing the inhalation to your belly. The chest should remain very quiet during this exercise. Use only your diaphragm. Many people, especially women, have inverted the in-breath and out-breath. Now is the time to correct the problem. Once again, inhale and the belly rises. Exhale and the belly drops. Keep your eyes closed through the entire exercise. Continue with slow and steady rhythmic breathing for a few minutes. When ready, begin the following gentle eye movements. As you inhale, while the eyes are still closed, lift them to the bridge of the nose. As you exhale, drop your eyes to your heart center. Continue for up to 5 minutes. When you become

more proficient, and your ocular muscles get used to the movement, try to extend your capacity. Lift the eyes to the eyebrow, and drop them to your navel. Then to the top of the head, and drop them to your feet. As you gain skill with reaching higher and lower, you will begin to expand into the greater light surrounding your physical body. You will feel more connected. More relaxed. This is especially good to do before sleep. The ocular movements stimulate the pituitary gland, which is associated with developing greater intuition. When the exercise has been completed, rest your awareness and your eyes in your heart center.

Part II

Chapter 6

"When his mind, intellect and self are under control, freed from restless desire so that they rest in the spirit within, a man becomes a Yukta - one in communion with God. A lamp does not flicker in a place where no winds blow; so it is with a yogi, who controls his mind, intellect and self, being absorbed in the spirit within him. When the restlessness of the mind, intellect and self is stilled through the practice of Yoga, the yogi by the grace of the Spirit within himself finds fulfillment. Then he knows the joy eternal which is beyond the pale of the senses which his reason cannot grasp. He abides in this reality and moves not therefrom. He has found the treasure above all others. There is nothing higher than this." *Bhagavad Gita* chapter 6

My journey into yoga began when I met my future teacher at a noon lecture while I was still working at the University. At the time, I was suffering from painful sciatica and hip pain and was taking ibuprofen 4 times a day. I had been to the spinal clinic, physical therapy, the chiropractor, and was receiving massages. In spite of these treatments nothing worked to relieve the pain. As I listened to this fellow speak during the lecture, I felt a growing interest in the idea of yoga. A physician friend of mine had given me a book of yoga postures way back in 1976. Between then and the time of the lecture the book sat on my bookshelf, unused. Occasionally I opened it to look at the photos. Skinny men sitting with crossed legs, holding their noses, looking up. Or, skinny men doing backbends and standing on their heads. It had not interested me.

But now I was in a different position. Not only was I willing to try something new because of the physical pain, but I also had the sense that this teacher had something to teach me. In hindsight it seemed one of those times of prearrangement mentioned earlier. My "inner" was responding to an "outer" signal of some kind. I also felt drawn to learning from this fellow because he was from India. So far I'd had little luck in finding anyone willing to teach me about a passion of mine, kundalini energy. For years I had been searching for more information on this sacred life force. I read Gopi Krishna's books describing his very extreme experiences with kundalini energy and read just about every other book I could find on the topic, which was not easy at the time. In the early 1990's most of the books were written by men on a topic which seemed secretive and hidden. I was trying to find explanations for some of the experiences I'd had as a kid which I never understood. My first memory of this lifetime was as a toddler, standing between my mother's legs, facing her while she was sitting in a chair at my neighbor's home. Mother was holding on to my hands, and I bent backwards so that my head tilted towards the floor. I felt a delicious heat spreading from my spine to the top of my head. I realized I was in the hands of my Earth mother but I *knew* she was not my real mother. My real mother was the flow of energy running up my back and out through my head. How can a kid know this? All my life the feeling of this spine energy has been with me, causing my body to tremble until the energy finds its way up and out. The man who was standing in front of the group talking about yoga was from the East. Surely those from the East had more knowledge of this sacred energy than those of us in the West. He would laugh today if he knew this was my ulterior motive for asking him to be my teacher. Always use caution when you ask someone to be your teacher! But it was ultimately this keen interest in learning more about my own kundalini energy that brought me into the fold of learning with this yoga teacher.

At the end of the lecture I obtained his phone number. That night I called him to set up an appointment. Days later, without warning, he showed up at my house at 7 pm with a bag full of groceries. Right then and there he prepared Tea: 4 cups whole milk, 4 cups water, 4 teaspoons sugar, 1/4 teaspoon crushed cardamom and 1 teaspoon gotu kola herb. He brought the milk to a boil and turned off the heat, added 2 teaspoons of black tea which steeped for 5 minutes, added a pinch of salt, and strained. Oh my god! The tea was delicious. After preparing and drinking the tea, he walked into my living room, sat down on the floor and started yelling the most primal sounds I'd ever heard. My husband disappeared up the stairs while I squirmed with discomfort. I was not used to the sounds he was making. Was it chanting? It was like nothing I had ever heard before, and it was so *loud*. I didn't know what to think. Should I tell him to leave immediately? "Ignorance prior to investigation" ran through my mind. I felt self conscious and I wanted to shush him immediately. What were my neighbors on the other side of the thin wall thinking? I decided to sit with him if for no other reason than to tell him he was making too much noise.

However, he was not one to be quieted. He proceeded to show me the hand postures, or grips, often called mudras, that correlated to the sounds he was making which were so unfamiliar to me at the time, and demonstrated a breathing technique called the 1-4-2 breath. When he was through with the cycle of sounds and breathing, he sat in silence. Before leaving he told me I had to start doing yoga poses. And that I had to drink the tea. And rise at 4 am to practice the breathing technique, mantra and mudra. And learn how to cook. And show up at his class. Oh, and there was the castor oil purge and fast, to be done every other month. Two tablespoons of castor oil with a glass of warm water at 7 am. A glass of warm water every half hour until 10 am. When you're hungry enough to eat a rug at 4 pm there is white toast with butter and tea. Spiced dal for dinner. Followed by two weeks of turmeric capsules to keep the gut clean. You had to know this fellow to appreciate his boldness. I said OK to everything.

I did not really know what I was getting into. Before long I found myself attending class three evenings a week. Thank you, Lois, for often being my yoga buddy. First we practiced the 1-4-2 breathing technique. Inhale to the count of 4, hold to the count of 16, and exhale to the count of 8. Any number divisible by 4 could technically be used, but we did not use a different variation in class. The inhale was particular in that the breath had to be brought up consciously from the abdomen to the chest, then expanded into the lungs, all the while lifting the eyes up and around the skull front to back. We had a twelve inch, oblong piece of styrofoam set against our backs, perpendicular to the back of the chair, that we leaned against to open our lungs and chest. I must say, sitting in this position I never felt more like a Marilyn Monroe impersonator in my life. Like most breathing techniques, the 1-4-2 breath technique brings oxygen to the body, expands the lungs, and provides stability to the mind. An important aspect of this technique, as taught by this teacher, was to simultaneously practice eye movements thus providing a link between the eyes and the breath. I've since learned specific movement of the eyes places pressure on and stimulates the upper glands - the pineal, and the pituitary. These are ductless glands situated in the head and are powerful tools for evolutionary growth. They are a connection to your divinity and in some circles would even be called your divine glands. In his book *Light On Life* Bellur Krishnamachar Sundararaja Iyegar writes that working with the frontal brain is working with analysis. But when we spread our ocular awareness from the back corner of the temple, near the ear, the back brain is brought into play and works with synthesis. The back brain is holistic and reassembles our awareness, bringing us greater sensitivity. At the time, little did I know the influence these glands would play in my future healing room.

When I first started practicing these ocular movements it was a strain because I had never used my eye muscles in that way before. Now it is second nature to me. I have come to believe in the importance of stimulating these glands in relationship to intuitive awareness. And it is my opinion that as we begin to learn more about consciousness we will place more emphasis on the pineal gland and its contribution to becoming more aware of Divine Presence. This type of practiced eye movement seems to be tremendously beneficial for the health of the eyes as well.

With the 1-4-2 breath I noticed an expansion in my lung capacity not known to me before. It was actually the first time in my life that I felt the influence of the alveoli, those tiny air sacs extending out from the lungs that contribute to the exchange of oxygen and carbon dioxide. I hadn't realized I had breath beyond my breath, inflation beyond what I had ever experienced. And it was a real practice for me to start using my diaphragm for proper breathing technique, which felt awkward and uncomfortable. Like most muscles in the body, the diaphragm becomes stronger with exercise. Watch any child while they are breathing and you will see their belly inflates with inhalation and deflates with exhalation. Later, once my healing practice was open, I was alarmed to notice almost all the women who had not received breath work training had inverted their breath cycle, as was the case with me. They inhaled and their belly deflated, they exhaled and their belly inflated. Additionally, there was a common pattern of using the upper chest as the breathing tool instead of the diaphragm. Men, on the other hand, were almost always in a normal breath cycle.

This tells volumes about what happens to women during the course of their lifetime, often as early as adolescence or puberty, to cause such a disruption in their normal breathing pattern. Anxiety, societal messages, holding in the stomach, emotional challenges, stress, fear, all can interfere with the normal breath cycle for women and girls. It is an egregious affront to women and we should all be made aware of this problem. Breath is power and life itself. I couldn't help but think a sinister and wily force had found a way to suppress the feminine energy by keeping it under the thumb of an overriding and dominant influence, thus dampening the power of the feminine. Perhaps that is my women's health nurse practitioner persona speaking, but I can tell you that once we corrected the breath patterns in women most of them had a good cry. The release of emotions was sometimes torrential. And engaging the diaphragm helped women to regain optimism and good health practices in addition to gaining confidence and belief in themselves. In the future, I will not at all be surprised when science discovers the connection between lung expansion and consciousness.

Back to yoga class. The yoga sounds were sung after the completion of the systematic technique of breathing. By nature, I tend to be on the quiet side. Except for my short lived and now ancient high school cheerleading career, I am not one to yell much. So learning the yoga "sounds" that coincided with the hand grips, or mudras, cost me about 45 years worth of Norwegian repression. YAAY. VAUE. RAAA. HAEE. LAOO. OM. These sounds were not whispered. They were forcefully projected with the animation of a lion. Think avalanche in the Himalayas. There was no tiptoeing into this practice. As a beginner,

I jumped feet first into the deep end of the vocal pool and put all my might into making the sounds. It was worth the price. I felt vibration from head to toe. The slumbering energy within me raised her sleepy head and took notice.

We started the yoga postures, or asanas, Iyengar style, after practicing the 1-4-2 breath technique, hand grips and sounds for twenty minutes. I had no idea then who Iyengar was. My teacher said Iyengar was a friend of his and indeed, he had a photo on the window sill of the two of them together at a yoga retreat in Chicago. They were smiling. Anyone who has ever studied with the revered master teacher can appreciate the work it takes to be a student of Iyengar. If you have looked through *Light On Yoga*, you will see he sometimes used his body weight to help another achieve an asana, which is what we often did in class. During the first week of yoga class I was introduced to an unconventional technique that is meant to release old hurts and pain from the body. My teacher instructed me to lie down face first on a cot that had been placed against the wall. Suspicion raced through my mind, but I did what was asked of me. No sooner was I lying face down when one of the other female students stepped up onto the cot and began to walk barefoot across my body. Like a cat kneading with its paws she went up and down my back, my arms, my thighs, knees and calves. Fortunately I didn't have to endure this for more than a few minutes because it was exceedingly painful. I didn't know if I should laugh or scream and was doing some of both. However, for the duration of my time with this teacher the back walking became a staple of the yoga class and it didn't take long for me to realize the great benefit it had on my body.

After the hour or so of asanas we went into the kitchen to cook. The bane of my existence then. This was grueling for me and I endured more wrath in the kitchen than I deserved from this teacher. He hollered that I should not be allowed in the kitchen! I felt like the beginner that I was, but kept at it. All these ingredients I had never heard of, spices I now had to cook with, recipes that were unfamiliar. While growing up my father could not tolerate anything more than salt and a little bit of pepper, and I seemed to have inherited his tender, Norwegian palette. So here I was, grinding coriander seeds, mustard seeds, cumin seeds, fennel seeds, ajwan seeds, poppy seeds, sesame seeds and every other kind of seed on the planet. I was dicing and seeding hot peppers, so foreign to me, soaking lentils, cooking rice, warming chapati on the gas stove, making combinations of ground spices to add to the heated oil. By the time we finally sat down to eat I was mentally and emotionally exhausted from the stress of learning and all the hollering, not to mention having worked all day. But the food made it all worth it. First the fragrant dal on the plate with the cooked, spiced vegetables. Yogurt to help with the heat. Warm chapati for scooping. Second helping, rice in the middle. More dal. More vegetables. More bread. So satisfying.

I was usually home by 10:30. Who ever heard of a four hour yoga class? Sometimes there were 2 or 3 of us at class, but often I was the only one. It was crazy and it was tortuous. But mostly it was healing.

I worked with that teacher 20 hours a week for 6 months. If I had not burned the copious notes I took during that time of learning I would include some of the details here. It was wild. So much happened so fast. To my teacher's credit, by the end of the six months I could do nearly every asana in the book *Light On Yoga*. I was practicing conscious breathing techniques three times a day. All back and hip pain disappeared. I felt like I had become a different person. The postures and breathing practices brought flexibility and healing to my body. It was truly a miracle to be feeling so healthy and pain free.

I wish I could say that I was able to keep up my relationship with this teacher, but I was not. In spite of feeling healed physically, the mental and emotional stress within the relationship became too difficult for me. That being said I am the first to recognize that deep emotions reside within the body and contribute to bodily dysfunction. I realized during those 6 months that this teacher did what he had to do to bring out the deep and mischievous feelings within me that were buried underneath the pain. There is tenderness in that recognition. One day I found the courage to simply write him a note telling him I needed a break. That was that.

I have seen him a handful of times since then and he occasionally shows up in my dreams. Without his assistance as "the opener" I would not be where I am today. While he never talked to me directly about kundalini energy, the methods he taught me were ones that lead to expression of this divine energy in profoundly satisfying ways. "Give a man a fish and you feed him for a day. Teach a man to fish and you feed him for a lifetime." As I was to later learn, the manifestations of this energy were about to lead me down an entirely new and creative path. What he taught me had come directly out of a book on kundalini practices printed in India, which I later obtained while traveling there.

So ultimately my teacher did know about this sacred life force and my hunch had been correct about him after all. I don't know what would have happened had I been able to keep up with due diligence a working relationship with him. What I do know is that I am deeply grateful to this teacher who had inner vision and was willing to extend himself for my growth. I learned that in spite of having the best teachers however, ultimately we are the ones who have to do the work if we intend to heal and grow. No one can do it for us. Love yourself enough to be willing to do the work.

Even though I stopped working directly with this teacher, for the next 30 months I rose at dawn, made tea, did the pranic breathing exercises, the mantras, the mudras, then meditation. I kept up with the practice of the asanas for two hours, three times a week. Truly

I was on my own now. I would not advise it, but that is how it played out. When the wild and intense meditation experiences started happening to me months later as a result of the practices I had learned, I kept them to myself. If I did try to explain them to others they would smile and say, "uh huh." But I knew they did not know what I was talking about. The meditations were so deeply personal and like something out of a fairy tale. Surely no one would believe they really happened and how could I explain them from a rational, western minded point of view? Going back to my yoga teacher felt senseless, as our relationship had not been one for intimate conversation. But I can tell you today that the meditative experiences were very real, and from a yogi's perspective, I suppose I earned them. I had expanded into a new reality not of this world and thankfully it eventually led me to find my destiny.

After calling it quits with my yoga teacher I noticed a longing to be in a yoga class. Since I was still working at the University, I found a kundalini yoga class on campus and a teacher there who was very supportive. I took his class for one year. It helped to calm my nerves and added balance to my practice. In my mind I thought for sure a kundalini yoga teacher would know about kundalini experiences, but for some unknown reason I felt too uncomfortable to approach him. So I will never know if that thought was true about him. When he moved to another State I tried going to other teachers but I guess I didn't try hard enough, because no one else could satisfactorily explain what was happening to me as a result of my meditation practices. I did find good information in the book *Kundalini Yoga for the West* by Swami Sivananda Radha, and I realize now that I had started to have spiritual experiences as a result of the deep yoga and pranayama practices that I had adopted. Human teachers are not very likely to define anyone else's truth for them, even when they are asked. Nonetheless, I longed to sit at a Guru's feet and have it all spelled out.

Eventually my meditations became my teacher and I began to rely on the Guru within. When I started the meditation practices, I was simply doing what my yoga teacher told me to do. I did not think much about them, nor did I enter into the practices expecting any outcome. To say I was naive is an understatement. But in spite of that naivety, or maybe because of it, I was transported during meditations to destinations most of us can only read about in sacred texts. I met Masters of Great Light and participated in otherworldly activities that were to be played out at a later time in my healing room. When I finally did open my healing practice the meditations reflected the progress I was making as a healer. That is, in my morning meditation, I would have an experience that prepared me for the work to be done in the healing room that day. It was the most amazing realization when I was finally able to make the connection that things really were being worked out on my behalf, and that I was receiving training on inner levels to fortify and inspire me.

I also realized, finally, that my meditations were for me to figure out, not for someone else to do so for me. I suspect it is the same for you. Mysteries cannot be scientifically picked apart and defined. They are meant to be appreciated and experienced, leaving us with a touch of magic that makes us smile. That being said, I would advise that if you really intend to become a seeker it is important for you to be in the fold of a reliable teacher who can help guide and direct you in your meditations and practices, and help maintain equilibrium as you open more deeply to your sacred, spiritual nature.

Indian Gota Kola Tea

Ingredients:

12 oz. whole milk (do not substitute fat free milk. Cholesterol is a required ingredient)

4 tsp. Indian cane sugar

2.5 tsp. black tea

salt to taste (1-cent heap suggested)

16 oz. water

1 tsp. gotu kola leaves

1/4 tsp. crushed cardamom seeds

Mix together in a stainless steel pot; milk, water, sugar, gotu kola leaves, and freshly ground cardamom. As the mixture approaches boiling, foam rises to the top. Reduce heat, add tea, and gently beat down the foam. Tea should not brew for more than five minutes. Add salt and strain. Drink it hot.

Chapter 7

"Don't tell me the sky's the limit when there's footprints on the moon." Paul Brandt

After ending my relationship with my yoga teacher, I proceeded to practice the meditation routine every day no matter the circumstances or company. Whether on a train headed to the Rockies or spending a weekend with my girlfriends or in the basement at my parents, the practice continued. I had been committed to the daily morning meditation, mantra, and mudra ritual for two and a half years when the first transcendent experience unexpectedly happened to me. During those two and a half years of meditation practice, my consciousness was undergoing major reconstruction. When I look back, I understand that on internal levels a seismic shift was occurring. The Life inside of me was carefully and systematically rearranging my psyche to accommodate the opening of my healing practice and attuning me to the sensitivities of the Helpers, who were still unknown to me. Here's how it came down.

My husband and I had just moved into a new apartment. It was early summer, shortly after resigning from my University position. I was experiencing tremendous freedom and excitement as the sole proprietor of my healing practice, which had been open for a few weeks. When we moved into the apartment, outside of our bedroom window was a huge, yellow scaffolding reaching from the ground, up past the height of the building. In the entire year we lived there, the scaffolding remained in place, but I never saw a workman on it. Earlier in this story I remarked that if we are paying attention, we will notice that internal changes are often reflected in our physical environment. Spirit sends us subtle and sometimes quirky signs as affirmation that our physical world coincides with our internal world. We cannot separate the two. I didn't know exactly what was happening when I saw that scaffolding, but seeing it stopped me in my tracks. There might as well have been a sign on it saying "Hello, I symbolize your upward growth and represent a bridge to higher worlds." I felt like I was about to go through an initiation of sorts, which carried willingness, but also a touch of dread. The scaffolding reached into the sky just as I was preparing to reach up into the sky of my own consciousness, and I somehow *knew* this. The ancient texts refer to the internal bridge as the"antahkarana", a Sanskrit term meant to describe a bridge that connects the lower mind with the higher mind, or soul. Through it an individual is able to realize profound love and wisdom, which transcends the rational, thinking processes of the lower self, or the personality. This bridge of light is said to be the medium used by the soul to communicate its love and purpose to the human mind. Through various spiritual disciplines, like the ones I had adopted, construction of that bridge is made possible. When built over time the antahkarana, also commonly called the "rainbow bridge", provides direct communication between the soul and the human personality. If I could be, or somehow was being, connected to this bridge of light, I was made aware of the support available to me as manifested by the strength of that yellow scaffolding.

Once again, I believe my hunch was right. My consciousness was about to change and so began a six month period of time when traveling outside of this dimensional existence became a common meditation experience for me. I guess you could technically call it "orientation", since it happened during the first six months of my healing practice. And I suppose you could say I was being trained by the Helpers, training which I definitely needed. The Masters, Guides, and Angels who appeared repeatedly in my meditations tried to teach me, on internal levels, the course of action we were to take in the healing room. Only in hindsight did I realize that my profound meditation experiences were being played out for me as a preview to our work together with my clients. And that my energy centers were being rearranged and prepared to minister to others in this new way. It also demonstrated to me, in retrospect, how slow my highly prized Western medical mind was to accept the new reality that my Inner Being had already comprehensively mastered so well. I could later see how ignorant I was of the power held in the sacred mantra, mudra and pranayama of my daily meditation practice, which became the communication vehicle used by my soul. I never dreamed of or expected the powerful experiences that were ahead of me. Perhaps that is precisely why they happened.

As a rogue yoga student, I had been gaining skill and experimenting with breathing techniques (pranayama)on my own. Chin lock, inhale 30, hold 30, exhale 30, hold 30. Inhale 60, exhale 60. Breath of Fire 5 minutes, 11 minutes, 20 minutes. Prana, the spirit energy within the breath, filled me up and became the foundational life force used to support delicate energy exchanges during healing sessions. During meditation, I was following the sacred kundalini teachings. When the mystical meditation experiences started happening, I took fastidious notes. Not only did I want to record them, but I was also looking to understand and explain what was happening to me. These days there are likely many qualified teachers who have experience working in higher dimensions and the study of kundalini who can help to safely expand ones consciousness into these greater awarenesses. No one should ever tell you to go off by yourself and practice strenuous pranayama. Even my yoga teacher cautioned me to not do more than twenty minutes of practice. But truth be told, I really didn't want anyone interfering with my experiences. I wanted to discover the mystery for myself. Over time my experiences became my truth. I tell the story to let you know what is possible. Not that you will necessarily have these experiences, but that you will value and trust the ones you have. We are extensive, beautiful, multilevel beings who are expected to contribute our creative abilities for the good of all living creatures. There is so much more to us that we see with the naked eye. It is truly time to expand into this awaiting nature where we gain access to greater knowledge, power and love. My consciousness was forever changed, and I had to change course with it.

The experiences I am about to share contributed to my inability to live and work in the world as I had previously existed. It enabled me to see beyond the physical realm and understand hidden meanings behind the human psyche. It allowed me relationship with a cadre of beautiful Beings who existed and stood in the wings at higher levels of consciousness within me - and within those of you who entered our healing room.

So I would ask you to read the words from my meditation experiences without applying judgement. They are written accurately and in simple language, as I had no other way to express myself. I remained unattached to religious teachings, though perhaps because of my childhood upbringing Jesus showed up several times in my meditations as a representative of the Christ Consciousness. I am leaving out the descriptive terms that hold judgement, like astral travel, etheric travel, quantum travel, etc. even though these terms may apply to my experiences. The terms are too limiting. I choose to believe that my Soul took charge of my destiny and used my meditation practice as a means to employ me as her beloved and to prepare me for our work together in the healing room. At the time, I felt all the meditative happenings were for the benefit of drawing me closer to the source of my existence. Whatever was happening to me was happening for a reason and it was assisting with my abilities as a healer. I absolutely trusted the process and did not resist. I worked to remain open minded and did not attach any allegiance to religion, denomination or culture. I did not want any limitation to my explorations. I surrendered to the energy and allowed myself to be carried in this current of love. During the first six months of opening my healing practice, I was being transformed on multiple levels, having visitations from multiple Beings of Light, and yet had to stay grounded, practical and levelheaded. Balancing these other worlds has become second nature to me now, but it has taken time to grow into the new me.

All of my conscious traveling experiences, in italics, happened during my meditation practice time in the morning with the exception of the first one, which occurred spontaneously one morning at dawn. Here it is, meditation number one.

> *I felt as though I were falling out of bed. I thought I was*
> *going to hit the floor, so I put my arms out to break my fall.*
> *I went down through the floor, came up, passed through*
> *the wall to the other side of the closed bedroom door, and*
> *found myself in the hallway. I was aware of my body*
> *and had complete mind ability. My eyes were focused and*
> *concentrated and I saw beautiful shapes and colors before*
> *my eyes. An image came into focus then that looked like*
> *a church steeple, or turret. As soon as the image formed, I*
> *was back in my bed.*

Now, this was not a dream. I did not dream about falling out of bed. I traveled with astute awareness. I was literally having a dual experience with my physical body. This was the beginning of my meditation experiences that continued for the next 6 months. As far as the image that formed before my eyes that morning? I believe it was a sign of things to come. Some weeks later I heard about a healing arts building that was to be built in Madison. My husband and I eventually became the caretakers of the new building that, when erected, had turrets just like the one I had been shown during my meditation experience. The future had been presented to me before it manifested in the physical world, which became a theme of my meditation experiences. Healing techniques were likewise demonstrated in my meditations. This brought reassurance to me, and a great measure of confidence. I felt encouraged and energized to keep up with the practices. I felt the presence of invisible Guides within my being, pushing me toward a great and irresistible light.

Since I was able to control my working hours, I chose a convenient schedule to start seeing clients which allowed plenty of time for early morning meditation. My husband was still working and he left the house at daybreak during the week. As soon as he left, I locked the door and began my practice. Anyone who's had a deep meditation experience will learn to lock the door. It is a reminder during the meditation that no outsider has entered the room and provides reassuring safety for the mind.

My morning routine was consistent. I was up at dawn to make the tea. While drinking the tea, I started the pranayama, or breathing exercises. Following the breath work came the singing of the sacred sounds with the mudras. Mudras, the hand postures, or grips, are used in yoga often in tandem with other practices, like breathing or chanting. They stimulate different parts of the body and affect the flow of energy within the body. The mudras I used, in conjunction with the sacred sounds, were meant to stimulate the energy centers, or chakras. Heart, kidney, rectum, navel, throat, third eye, crown. The entire practice would take about a half hour, depending on the depth of the breath work I chose for that day. I always practiced while sitting up. Eventually I experimented with lying down after the practice, and that position brought a more deeply relaxed body for the Spirit to use as a vehicle for traveling. Some might call this resting time shavasana - others may say it was samadhi. I would call it paradise.

Profound blessings and spiritual experiences came to me then, during this meditative resting time. I retained my consciousness and complete awareness, and even my body. But I was entirely weightless. All words fail to express the rapturous, joyful feeling of weightlessness. And I traveled at what seemed like the speed of light until I reached a destination. I realized these destinations were within myself, within my chakra system, and that, from our third dimensional reality, I really didn't go anywhere. But it was absolutely exhilarating. This is the vastness of consciousness. You may recall in the movie, "Cosmos", based on Carl Sagan's book, when the astronaut (actor Jody Foster) was in the space craft. She took the journey through space while those who were observing reported to her later that she never left the launching pad. This was a real experience for her, through space, and to another place - a planet, actually. Those in observance saw nothing. This is a great description of consciousness exploration. One's experience may be nothing like another's, just as mine was for me. If someone had witnessed my body, they would have said I never left the couch. Yet, there I was on a journey, meeting Angels, Masters and Guides, traveling at warp speed through buildings and walls, shouting holy names into the darkness, accompanied by tremendous Spiritual Beings, having my energy centers rearranged, and feeling the incredible influence of great Teachers as they stood beside my resting body. Oh, the love of it all.

You would have to verify it with my husband and others who were around me at the time, but I think I remained reasonably grounded and sensible in my daily life in spite of the wild meditation experiences. That in itself was a miracle. Coming back from ecstatic experience holds potentially overwhelming hazards that can derail the most seasoned expert. That is exactly why we do our practices. So we can apply them in our daily lives when things become challenging, and that includes coming back from the bliss.

Part III

Chapter 8

"All I'm saying is that to liberate the potential of your mind, body, and soul, you must first expand your imagination." Robin Sharma

The meditation experiences I am about to introduce to you were happening for a while before I started recording them. Better late than never, as they say. Here are a handful of them taken from my journal, unedited, deeply intimate, and straight from the heart. They all happened during the resting time after the yoga, mantra, pranayama practice while lying down. Meditation number two.

In my mind there is complete light, complete silence of the mind, complete oneness, warmth, peace in the body. There is nothing but light. In the meditation I am sitting up. A Being comes down the hallway towards me. There is no speaking. Understanding happens without using words. I welcome him. He sits in front of me as though on a stool, and we begin to interact as friends - warmly, lovingly. I am advised to stretch backward and as I do so it feels as though my middle is somehow being parted and I sense either a pouring in or the swallowing of a liquid with a very bitter, pungent taste. I mentally comment that I feel like vomiting, and indeed have a sense of retching. The Being is calm, reassuring. I understand a healing is being done for me and I experience a shudder of dread as I realize this. These are always quite painful, not so much physically but they illicit an emotional response in addition to deep visceral discomfort, which is not unlike physical pain. I feel, then, an urge to contort to the right, yet a part of my body is actually turning the opposite way, sort of like the motion of wringing something out, squeezing from opposite directions. This creates a deep discomfort, not really painful, but deeply sad, and I feel tearful and again nauseated. I begin to retch and gag but nothing actually comes out of me. The motion/emotion of release/gagging stimulates the energetic removal of whatever is diseased on my mid to right side. Whether this is kidney or liver or muscular injury I do not know. It is not revealed to me, although my sense is it's my right kidney related to an old illness or injury. I ask to be comforted by the Angelic Beings who are assisting and who are beside my head. I relate silently with appreciation for their devotion and care. They understand my discomfort, physically and emotionally.

I am glad not to have been forewarned. I comprehend the energetics of this type of healing, but in my very limited wisdom cannot see into my body well enough to know exactly what needs healing. I feel my Teacher/Guide sees my perfection, as is the case in our healing room with our clients. I ask to be healed on a cellular, biologic level, and these Beings respond in kind. It is a matter of supply and demand. After the retching subsides, I wipe my tears and feel a lightness, a release. The Master Light Being in charge of the healing then checked my channels to see if they were balanced. He used energetic light from the bottom chakra up to the middle. It spun there for a bit and moved on up to my throat, brow and crown. It was released through my head and came up under me again. He was satisfied with the results, and pleased. I felt wonderfully refreshed after this meditation experience.

Bit by bit, my level of understanding was growing and enabled me to calmly and cooperatively interact on levels not usually available to most of us. I became used to being in the moment of the meditation experience without the interference of my rational mind. Having a reprieve from the pressure of the mind, even for a short period of time, was in itself, an oasis. Only later, when the experience was over, did I try to apply logic to help put the pieces together. I wondered who came to visit me in this meditation and if this Entity doing the healing might be an aspect of myself from the future. It's a perfect illustration that from the Helpers' perspective, it seemed less important to know "who" and more important to know "what." They never, ever focused on Themselves. Their attention was always for the benefit of others.

Slowly, I was realizing the experiences during meditation coincided with the learning in my healing room. At that time, in the very beginning, I was not familiar with the energy techniques demonstrated in meditation. I was again reminded in this particular meditation that pain residing within the body is not always the direct result of a physical injury. "The body never forgets" was a phrase my yoga teacher used often as he told me over and over that everything is recorded within the body on all levels - physically, emotionally, and mentally. I shed many tears holding a yoga asana that felt physically comfortable yet extracted a great deal of emotional pain. Such is the power and wisdom of yoga. This meditation reinforced and affirmed what I had been witnessing in the healing room as well. When working to mend a physical problem, clients shed tears of sadness, loss, or loneliness. Today I feel quite safe in saying it is very rare to have a physical injury without acquiring an emotional or mental tagalong. They happen simultaneously and if you think about your own injuries, you will see that you suffered from an intense feeling when the injury or illness happened. This is an aspect of healing often overlooked in the traditional Western medical model. You can't put a cast or a brace on a feeling. The Invisible Helpers were training me to lift my hands from the physical body into the subtle bodies surrounding it where emotional and mental traumas can cause great disturbance if not treated properly.

I was being guided in the healing room to "pour" liquids into a chakra center, or to ask a client to imagine they are "swallowing" a liquid as had been demonstrated to me in this meditation. Indeed, when I asked the client to tell me the color of the liquid they were receiving, most often they were able to give me one. It thrilled me beyond measure to hear the client participate in this way because, after all that had been revealed, I was still skeptical.

Chapter 9

"It is a fire of awareness which burns ignorance so that life takes on a new meaning and all previous concepts are burned up. It turns the individual upside-down into a new being." Swami Sivananda Radha on Kundalini Fire.

Meditation number three.

In my mind, I follow a Guide who is holding a flame. He takes me down many steps, way, way down. I can feel we are near the bottom of my chakras. All the way down to the base center, which feels quite rapturous and delicious.

It feels like there are men there. Also a large figure sitting perhaps on a throne - lots of hair and beard, like Zeus or a lion. There are snakes all around the floor. I sit, then lie down with them and allow them to move through my chakra centers. In and out, from bottom to top. I feel in love with the snakes, as though my body is processing for these snakes and opening to them. It is like a dance. Soon all the snakes are gone. The floor is empty. Where there had been masses of snakes, there are now none. The ceremony is over. All is quiet. My sense is that these snakes represent all the women who will open to kundalini through our healing room and through their I AM. Hundreds, perhaps thousands of women. The snakes were released through me.

Kundalini energy, my eternal companion. An energy so subtle as to be imperceptible to the majority of people. The Sanskrit word kundalini means coiled, like a snake. When awakened, she is said to contain humankind's potential. Evolving kundalini energy is as natural as human existence. It animates our very lives. It is not recognized by medical science per se, and is often misunderstood even among yoga practitioners and teachers. Most of us are not aware of this divine flow of energy within us. But for me, it has been a constant and ever present reminder that I am attached to a life force greater than myself. It has provided me access to an inner connection, even as a kid. While the history of kundalini has been cast as a very mysterious and potent energy, a softer truth was exposed in our healing room. We relied on the energy of kundalini to cleanse the chakras and used it to create pathways for deeper relationship to the Self. This was not my idea. It was the method brought to the healing room by the Helpers. It was a very natural and normal part of all healing sessions. We worked with kundalini energy gently and safely via the breath, which supported its movement. Kundalini is essential when working with the light body. It is, in fact, the foundation for establishing ourselves as cosmic beings.

Kundalini can be specifically aroused, or "awakened", from its slumber at the base of the spine by intense meditation or breath practices. Those who are successful and safely arouse their kundalini are said to gain a great partner on their spiritual journey. I believed this partner existed in my healing room and was revealing the etheric team of Healers assisting with our new work. These meditations in particular represented to me the powerful and vital use of kundalini energy, now a lifeline to my destiny. This energy is our birthright. It is within us and as close as our heartbeat. We are her and she is us. Let us not resist.

Over the next few days I had a second meditation that seemed to express the gloriousness of the energy working within my channels of Light. Here it is, meditation number four.

I traveled, and used my body a lot. Ice skating was lovely. Zooming through space, my legs dangling beneath me in the wind. Total freedom and deliciousness. Toward the end I was walking in a natural field somewhere, then riding in a jeep with two men in the front seat. One of them owned the nature preserve. The other was a consultant. I was feeling pulsating vibration in my second chakra. All the while in the meditation I am aware that I cannot see with my physical eyes because my pupils are not functioning. Therefore, I cannot see in the world of function at all. It causes a bit of stress during the meditation because I think I am with other people, supposed to be doing something else I will have to be accountable for. I remind myself I am in the meditation. (This is the purpose of locking the door, and thus remembering during the meditation, so I can remind myself I am safe in my room. It will give me more freedom). At one point in the meditation, I was lying in the grass and I could see myself from above. I had my hands in the air and they were bent towards me. I had been hollering something. Towards the end of the meditation, as I was riding in the back seat of the jeep, the pulsing in my second chakra was becoming so powerful it was all I could concentrate upon. It was what I would call "erotic consumption" for lack of a better term. I was aware that the sensation was not accessible anywhere from the outside. It was inside me and gaining momentum. I was engaged in focused breathing, perhaps the breath of fire. Now the intention was all in the third eye, which gave strength and rhythm to the second chakra. As the vibration gained impetus, I put my attention back in the second chakra, actively participating with the energy until the vibration peaked and exploded into a profoundly glorious and satisfying release of beautiful color through my third eye and a pleasure beyond description in the physical body. When the third eye opened as the energy crested, I saw, and concentrated upon, a very beautiful cloud the color of fuscia. Inside of it was the word Love which then changed into a heart. I watched the heart take on the vibration of the second chakra and it started to pulse in rhythm with the magnificent vibration. The two centers were vibrating together - one unified pulse. Strangely, little icons like exclamation points and question marks appeared all around the heart. Then ever so briefly I saw many beings inside a cloud, all different shapes and sizes and of different professions. They looked like cartoon characters, actually. One had a nurses cap on. They were smiling and saying hello to me. I was told they were my Guardian Angels. Then I came out of the meditation and was back in my room.

Chapter 10

"I have been a seeker and I still am, but I stopped asking the books and the stars. I started listening to the teaching of my soul." Rumi

This exquisite conscious meditation came to me after a healer called and asked me to do a long distance healing on her because she had broken her hip. Distance healing, often referred to as non local healing, is a term used when the client is not directly in your physical space. Today I understand the logistics of them, but at the time I was a long way from having confidence in my non local healing skills. This meditation demonstrated specific methods of healing that had been emerging while working with clients. Because I was so focused on energetically reorganizing myself to accommodate the profound changes presented in my healing room - think Chicken Little believing the sky is falling - I didn't immediately realize the meditations were for my benefit to show me techniques used by the Helpers. Here is my account of her healing, meditation number five.

Frannie was lying in a bathtub of sandalwood and crystals. The consciousness of Jesus came in to do a healing for her. I saw that Frannie's pelvis was riddled with shards of glass - shattered pieces of glass, so much of it. I knew I could not walk in there because if I did so, the glass would become more deeply embedded. I waited and requested help. That's when Jesus then came in from my left side, a perception of his entire image - knowing it was him. He brought his hand to the area of shattered glass across Frannie's hip bones and held it there for a long time. He used Love to attract the shattered slivers of glass to his hand. They were drawn to him - magnetized to him. He said nothing, simply stood in Love. Eventually his whole being was covered with glass. He silently moved away from Frannie to a place of safety and stood there. I pondered the situation, and then realized that he was protected from the effects of the glass, like a divine Pied Piper. I wondered how he would rid himself of all the glass shards, and again he waited patiently until the glass simply fell off of him. This is like the actions taken in my healing room when we magnetize and then remove shards of negative energy from my clients. He had a loving, tender, deeply compassionate attitude toward the glass and was intent on preserving it. In my healing room, I stand and eventually release too, completely trusting that Helpers will come to remove what is being shed by my clients. I trust Them to dispose of the released energy properly and in alignment with the highest good. I see now that nothing is discarded in this meditation, no matter how shattered or threatening. It is honored and loved, even the broken shards of glass. Then Jesus returned to Frannie's pelvis and poured some kind of liquid or water over her pelvis. The liquid reacted with a black-like powder, which had already been placed in the pelvic area. From this chemical reaction rose a vapor and the powder began to bubble. This soon evaporated and the black substance turned into a sticky tar-like matter, which solidified and held the fracture in place. Jesus then moved up to the left rib cage, circulated energy round and round, and a white substance was used there, like calcium

or chalk. He energized the second chakra with golden light
and vibrational healing. Then the healing was over and
the images of Frannie and Jesus dissolved.

I was full of questions. I was seeing a healing acted out in my
conscious meditation exactly as I'd felt it happening in my healing
room. But in my healing room I was the one doing the healing. How
was this possible? I did not have knowledge of alchemy and surely this
was a style of healing one would not learn about in the books. Certainly
I hadn't. But that's exactly where I turned to try to figure out what was
happening. Great masters will tell you to question everything, but I say,
blessed are those who take what's given and ask no questions. It is so
much easier! Once again I was witnessing simultaneous stories in more
than one world, but this time I realized the story was a demonstration
to help ease my doubts. Like many healers, once in the healing room
I became the open door for the work. That is the benefit of surrender.
Yet my outer mind could only handle so much of the spectacular.
Imagine trying to describe the color red to someone who is blind. That
is how it felt for me to be in the midst of the great Energy Attendants
in my healing room and those who showed up in my meditations. The
expression and extent of the radiant nature of love and compassion held
within this Circle of Healers was like nothing I had ever experienced
or could ever describe. Not only was I now witnessing extraordinary

visuals in lucid meditation, but I was also becoming changed in my heart. I started feeling tremendous waves of compassion. So much so that I felt cramps in my heart.

When compassion comes to lay her head in the lap of the heart, the edges fall away and there is no boundary to contain its radiance. Like lava running down from the mountaintop, compassion will dissolve everything in her path. I had to learn how to stand in the power of this compassion. Dare I say, what better teacher could a girl have than Jesus. Some days my knees were weak from the enormous weight of it. In the healing room I had to learn how to wait, to stand by until the quality of compassion balanced whatever it was up against. There was no telling how long it would take. In that way, it made my job easier. It helped me to know "I" was not doing the healing - compassion was doing the healing. I just had to learn how to discern the vibrational time compassion needed to get the job done. This was a learning curve for me and often mirrored changes in the physical world. I became more likely to allow another to shine and stand in their own radiance. I was less likely to interfere and more likely to let nature take its course. From my experience I have learned there is nothing higher in vibration than compassion. It is the divine tipping point. Consuming all negativity, she has the ability to gently undress, then bless, all opposition

As the conscious meditations continued, I became more aware of the dynamic energy systems available to me as a healer. My work with the yoga teacher brought my body into balance. But the meditation practice and pranayama created an expansion of my consciousness and mind, bringing utterly fantastic, incomprehensible experiences to me during meditation.

The next meditation, number six, reminded me of an image I had received soon after opening my healing room, and remains with me to this day. The image reflected a perception of my healing table as a radiant, crystalline platform existing within a chamber of Light. Ancient beings adorned and worked within the chamber. For some reason, perhaps because of my ardent studies, on this particular morning I was feeling just about as weary of seeking as a spiritual seeker could get. I guess I really needed that adorned chamber.

> *I am taken to a Faraway place, looking for the God I know who resides there, but I finally have to stop when I realize there is no end to my journey. So I wait for God to find me. And God does find me. I am carried to the top of the stairs, many stories high, and placed face down across a rejuvenating seat - or a healing seat of some kind. I receive Light - restoration. I become the Light. My heart bursts open, expands, and there is no end to the expansion, for Love is consuming everything. Its strength outshines all darkness in the entire Universe, the way is cleared for safe transport home. The words I AM THE WAY THE*

> *TRUTH THE LIGHT flash across my vision. Instantly I*
> *am back in my living room.*

Meditation number seven, below, was also restorative. There is nothing like the feeling of traveling at light speed to raise one's vibration above the level of mental chaos that is caused by too much thinking. Meteoric travel with my body was a common and luxurious experience that occurred over and over during my conscious meditations. It brought tremendous relaxation to my body and mind. This particular meditation would later prove to be one that changed the course of my work and healing practice as I knew it.

> *I was flying fast and high, my arms and legs dangling in*
> *the warm atmosphere going so fast, yet I could see hundreds*
> *of Angels. They seemed to be stationary, and I was moving.*
> *Each one of them was smiling at me. I was trying to say hello*
> *to as many as I could, but was moving past them so fast it was*
> *impossible to greet each one. I felt in complete bliss and my*
> *body was one with everything. It was the end of all my desires.*

There was a period of time during my meditations when I heard distant bells, or gongs. It was as if someone was outside pulling the rope to ring the church bell and it was always in the upper left hemisphere of my brain - rhythmically for five or six rings - although I'd not really counted. No doubt it was the opening of a chakra, but it reminded me of what my birth mother told me about my actual birth, which coincided with the ringing of the 9 am church bells to signal that the Sunday service was about to begin. I suppose stranger things have happened than to remember one's birth, like having these meditations that just seemed to be getting more and more complex. In my studies of the chakras, I had been trying to piece together information from multiple sources to come up with an understanding of the lower energy centers in particular and how they related to the heart center. Again, I wanted to find out for myself rather than read what others had to say about this. While the following meditation, number eight, didn't especially help me to mentally clarify the information, it helped my psyche immensely. My spiritual nature took over during this meditation and carried information from one energy center to the other. And for that I am deeply grateful.

> *I could see into the lower centers, the nature groups of fairies,*
> *gnomes, elves, deeply scented pines, open meadows, fields,*
> *water, streams with branches bending over them, little*
> *Beings in the trees, on the ground, in the tree trunks, in*
> *openings at the base of trees, all over there were little Beings.*
> *I asked for a guide to come to lead me forward. I had a*
> *sense that these little ones were about to be connected to Star*

Beings. A guide came up the stairs, up and out the belly button space, and I silently spoke of my observation. We then walked together back down the stairs - not too far - it was more outward than inward, and he commented that it wasn't as far as I thought. When I arrived, I cried because I could see the Star Beings were already with the Nature Beings and it was so beautiful. They had been reunited. Sharing, touching, loving, and interacting together. The Star Beings were bigger, and were even holding some of the Nature Beings. I had the realization that the Star Beings were going to be taking the Nature Beings up the steps, and that is precisely what happened. As they walked up the solar plexus to the heart they all dropped out of sight, like they dropped off the planet. I felt a moment of panic that I had done something wrong since they disappeared so quickly yet I sensed they weren't really gone at all. I think they had been "dropped" or "placed" somewhere in a secure chamber behind my heart. I could feel them in the depths of my middle. Then the meditation went on to include a sense of bliss and peace. I checked in at the lower level and some of the Nature Beings were still there, yet the image of the Star Beings coming to their rescue was still obvious and present in my mind. Also, as the Star Beings were entering the Nature

Beings, the Nature Beings were relieved, and I cried again because they had been waiting for thousands of years to receive such help. They had been carrying the load alone.

Let me be the first to say, I do not really know what a Star Being looks like, but that is the term used in my writing when I returned from the meditative state. I seemed to know and recognize them during the meditation. It was common for me then to meet all varieties of Beings during these meditative trips. Lest you think I was using mind altering drugs during this time, I can assure you that I have never tried them. Even during the sixties when they were plentiful, much to my accumulated regret, I did not imbibe. This was my mind in its pure state, riding the winds of the practice, at the mercy of the universe.

I learned to follow the energy without reservation. A Guide or Angel merged with me, I allowed it, and surrendered. Stripped of my well established concepts, I became willing to take risks that molded the development of my mind to reveal new and extraordinary dimensions. My yoga teacher told me I was too "open" and perhaps that was true. Nonetheless, that opening left me with a yearning to pierce whatever limiting boundary was imposed or imagined by another's opinion - and my own. I had to find my truth for myself. The twelve step program I adopted along the way taught me to always talk things over with a spiritual advisor. And I have done so for the majority of my adult life. However,

I was running out of prospects who had traveled the same highway, and the more I tried talking to others about my meditation experiences, the quieter they became during our discussions. No doubt a psychiatrist would have had a hay day examining my mind. Had I traveled to an ashram I likely would have found kindred souls, but I didn't want to step away from my healing room. Internally I trusted I was being guided down the right path, but I did see a psychologist during that time, which was most helpful. Aside from an occasional raised eyebrow, he provided a safe environment for my wailing and reassured me that I was quite sane. Please don't ever hesitate to see a professional to help you sort out your worries. If you are willing to lay all your messiness on the table you will likely be rewarded with great relief and the possibility of new beginnings.

And it really was just that for me. I was at the point of no return. Profoundly changed on so many levels, physically, mentally, emotionally, spiritually, and now most likely biologically, I could no longer claim to be the same person I had been a year ago. My body was demanding certain requirements to sustain its mental clarity, and I had to learn how to respect and foster the new changes. It was not easy to grow discipline around these requirements. For example, after a while I was no longer processing sugars the way I used to. All blood tests were normal. There was no diabetes, blood sugars were stable, yet when I consumed sugar all manner of trouble started, from heart palpitations to sleeplessness to body cramps. My body was ready to have me stop cold turkey but I had to slowly wean myself off of this lifelong addiction. It broke my heart to say "no" to my mother's lemon meringue pie, chocolate brownies, cookies, ice cream, chocolate, treats. You wouldn't believe the amount of pressure others can put on you when you go against the grain of social norms and say "no" to their food! What I noticed through this ordeal was that my body had made a decision long before my mind was ready to accept it. The span of time between the body's decision and my ability to take action was quite delayed. Today when I receive a message from my body, I am much more able to make the correction quickly. It has taken years of practice to respect my body in this way, standing up for myself under the pressure of others who would have me behave or eat according to their specifications. My prayer coming through this writing is meant to go directly into your heart when I say to you, eat according to your body requirements. There is no "one size fits all" body type. Each one of us is as unique as our fingerprints. Do not eat something just because your siblings or your spouse or your friends are pressuring you to do so. Find the courage within to say no. You are worth it.

Stand up as you recite this affirmation mantra.
CLose your eyes and allow the words to penetrate your entire body.
I AM AN IMPORTANT AND WORTHWHILE PERSON.
I HAVE THE RIGHT TO STAND UP FOR MYSELF
AND ACT IN MY OWN BEST INTERESTS.

Chapter 11

"Fly me to the moon and let me play among the stars.

Let me see what spring is like on Jupiter and Mars."

Bart Howard

I had been reading Eknath Eswaran's *Love Without End* and was contemplating the idea of a God being with me, around me, and in me, so therefore I always had support. This meditation, number nine, actively demonstrated to me the feeling of support.

In my awareness I started to go into what has become a familiar clockwise rotation, spinning as fast as the force of a speeding train. My mind is not spinning and things around me are not spinning. But my physical body is taking my awareness with it, and we are rotationally and rapidly spinning in concentric circles, mostly clockwise. I do not resist, though there is a momentary panic about a hundred miles back. Then I am hurled through an opening. I surrender to the experience and go with the energy. I feel as though I cannot budge, as I am trying to move my physical body while lying on the couch but I am under the influence of centrifugal force. The meteoric pace finally lessens and I am out in space. I quickly pass through the stars. I have a slow motion experience then, as I pass through this void, an exquisite sensation of complete support no matter which way my body turns. Forward, backward, side to side, summersault. The feeling of being supported without a physical barrier to hold me up is so spectacularly lovely, which I am now getting used to. I am trusting that I will be supported in this "'space cushion" or whatever words can be used to describe the feeling. Then suddenly I am in water. And I go deep, deep, deep into the water, again faster than the speed of a train or plane and it takes a long time to get to the bottom. There is no consideration of physical breath, as it is of no concern.

Again the sensation of being held is constant. When I reach the bottom, there is Light. I place my left hand on, then into, the grains of sand on the floor of the ocean, and I see my hand glistening in the Light and see and feel the sand falling between my fingers. Then I am again spinning, spinning, spinning, which is so thoroughly enjoyable as an ecstatic experience. I surrender and allow the energy to carry me. Again I relax into this powerful force, and find myself returning to the space/void, which now takes a long time to pass through.

I am aware that I am alone in this very vast space I am zooming through, so I begin to decree. I use a strong voice and all my concentration and become the voice of the Mother God. As I am traveling through the darkness - void - space - I am clearly shouting "In the name of the Father, Son and Holy Spirit'" and "I come as the Mother God", "' I Am the Mother God", "In the name of the Father, Son and Holy Spirit", "I Am the Mother God'". On went the recitations, until enough was said. Then again, the slowing down and the exquisite tenderness of complete support without structure. As in the past, I have an awareness of someone in the room with me except now there seems to be talking. I experience a quick inner tap on the forehead. I realize in this quantum meditation that I am still going to go to another place, and I understand this is a longer time than I have previously experienced in deep meditation. So I again start the centrifugal motion, but this time it is similar to a motor starting - the sensation is like pulling on the rope to start a lawn mower, it goes around and around and then "catches." From then on, there is a steady hum as the motor is "running". I realized that I was actually in a motorized vehicle which was a part of me, and I lifted off from the ground and started going through space again. I could see that I (although now I had a sense of we) was approaching a planet, and I looked away momentarily because I felt such anguish and despair and shouted out, though I do not know if my human voice was working. Then, as we approached the planet, I could see that it looked like Earth, and I had an awareness that this was significant as space ships, indeed, were coming to Earth.

I was back on my couch, fully alert, although it took a while to assimilate and adjust back to this reality. The meditation lasted 30 minutes. I have no opinion on the possibility of "space ships", space brothers and sisters, or any spacecraft visitations to our home called Earth. I wrote the comment because I am reporting my experiences and it emphatically came through my meditation. It is what it is. I have had a big enough hurdle to jump over coming to terms with belief in the Helpers in my healing room. Here's what I do know. We are vast and expansive human beings connected to our stars and planets. We cannot separate ourselves from this planetary existence. For all I know, a space craft whizzed past, found me wandering around in outer space and kindly brought me home.

The practices I had adopted served a dual purpose. They provided coping strategies to help ground me in my daily life and now they were broadening my mind to new discoveries on inner planes of existence. They ultimately enabled me to learn more about being in partnership with my Universe. My consciousness was expanding and I had to trust the wisdom of my Inner Guidance. I was in unchartered waters. This meditation seemed particularly interesting to me because of the use of words put forth as I traveled through the void. I was invoking and anchoring the names of the Mother and the I AM, a vocal demonstration of what I had been learning through my studies. I was reading books on esoteric philosophies, the works of Alice Bailey, the Theosophical Society, Thomas Merton, Swami Sivananda Radha and the AMTF (Ascended Master Teaching Foundation) materials, among many others, trying to find clues to help solve some of the mysterious happenings in my healing room and meditations. My prior vision had established within me a picture of the Holy Ones standing under the umbrella of the one Source. If the Holy Ones under that umbrella were among the Helpers in the healing room, and They were there to act in service to my clients, were They there as Intermediaries from that Source? Were They working to ultimately expose hidden aspects of my client's indwelling natures, that they could know themselves as divine beings also directly under the umbrella of the one Source?

If so, I wanted to follow the ribbon of light that wound its way up to Source, and then keep that route open as a means of connection and travel. During sessions, I was aware of a pathway of Light directly above the clients that went far beyond my reach. The substance that I magnetically retrieved out of that Light held amazing and restorative qualities which were then reflected back to the client through their heart center. The information I was piecing together from my studies required me to step out of my prior belief system, which thus far had been shattered and turned completely upside down, and keep an open mind. It had already been shown to me that so much was possible. I knew now that I was being taught on inner levels to work in this new way with clients, and I tried to stay as neutral as possible to keep the door open for Spirit to enter. Was it a dangerous time for me, psychically, to be between the worlds in this way? When I shouted into the void and called on the Mother and the I AM, I had the sense of danger. Like whistling in the dark, was it a way of reassuring myself? Or was I truly being a loudspeaker for those Names to be forever etched within my aura as a mode of transport for divine nature?

I finally found information in my reading materials that connected the dots for me, with explanations that I now could understand. As foreign or complicated as it may sound, I found the reasoning to be a perfect match to what I had been experiencing during healing room sessions. The explanation came to me after the fact. And because of that, I adopted this reasoning as my new truth. Many esoteric teachings, particularly the AMTF, describe the human being as having not one, but seven bodies. Four lower bodies: the physical, the emotional, the mental, and the etheric. And three upper bodies: the High Self, sometimes referred to as the Christ Consciousness or one's Higher Consciousness, the Causal body, which contains the pure quality of Love, and the presence of the I AM. This confirmed what I felt had become true for me after opening my healing practice, as I was intuitively working in all of these bodies during the course of a session. But we placed particular emphasis on the three upper bodies, opening pathways of connection and energy exchange from the lower to the upper ones. The three upper bodies provided spiritual nourishment and respite via the chakra system from the intensity of the emotional, mental and physical stress within the four lower bodies and presented the pathway for Self realization. "In the name of the Father, Son and Holy Spirit" was a phrase I was prompted to use during sessions to anchor healing qualities and affirm a stable flow of energy between the client, their High Self, and their I AM. The pure substance of the Mother made this flow possible.

Like many of us, I'd heard those mysterious words spoken in the Lutheran church when I was a kid. When I first started saying them in my healing room, I was uncomfortable because I didn't want my clients thinking I had anything to do with religion or a prescribed God. I had formed an abstract idea of those words way back then and hadn't given them any thought for decades. But this new understanding was presenting an entirely different interpretation for me. During a healing we used those words to bless and integrate the unity within the clint's energy body. The Mother energy became the tool for weaving and connecting this unity of the upper and lower bodies and fueled my passion for the healing work. She became the Great Mover, the true Life Force moving through all time and space. In the healing room I repeatedly worked in an area above the client's crown center and as we asked the client to lift their awareness into that space, I was prompted to speak those holy words thus empowering and giving authority to a higher source of interconnectedness for the client.

As I report my experiences in this writing, I have to say that after careful study and evaluation, this explanation of the seven bodies has become my truth. Over time I realized the Helpers were involved in working to integrate and unite the consciousness of the four lower bodies to that of the three upper bodies, and the swinging door I had to continually walk through was the connecting one between those two worlds. This connecting door is sometimes referred to as the etheric body. I believe this was the fourth dimensional work I was supposed to be doing with the Masters. The etheric body was the point where I stood with the Helpers, remarkably having one foot in each world, magnetizing and radiating strands of light from the Lower to the Upper, while the client put forth the priceless effort of willingness. I have shared my truth with others, and even taught classes based on my experiences. However, I would never be so bold as to say one should believe as I do, nor would I impose my beliefs on another. You deserve to find your own truth. For a long time in my adult life I was a professed agnostic. No one could tell me what to believe, but a lot of folks tried. I eventually outgrew agnosticism and formed a belief in a Higher Power. My belief system now cuts an inclusively wide swath across the cosmos. I AM and the Great Mother remain my inspiration. No one ever came in to see me who was not connected to energy beyond their physical body. Everyone had the same connection to greater Source whether they believed in it or not. I suppose I could be imagining it, but I believe I am not. The naming or not naming of that Source is up to you.

Since its inception, it has been my obsession to find a way to truthfully express the healing room activities in terms that are understandable. It would have been so much easier if someone had simply passed me a note one day, spelling it all out in detail, explaining to me what I would be doing with the Masters. Instead, like most of us, I had to discover it for myself. As my old friend Burt used to say, we are here on Earth to learn our lessons. His saying rang true for me.

Chapter 12

"I have found the paradox, that if you love until it hurts, there can be no more hurt, only more love." Mother Teresa

"A new command I give you: Love one another. As I have loved you, so you must love one another." Jesus Christ

The Great Mother appears, Jesus exists as pure Love, the rays of the rainbow are revealed, and I am included in the circle of devoted Yogi's. I put this meditation into words, but my words are woefully inadequate to help explain the ambiance and experience of being in the presence of such great Light. Please excuse my deficiencies in this regard. My only other option would have been to remain silent, and as you know by now, that is no longer my desire.

I would never claim to have reached the top of the spiritual summit, for I still have a long way to go. But if there had been a layover on the way up during my time of ardent seeking, this is the place I would have chosen to rest - here in meditation number ten.

I sat in a field, next to a tree. Beside me sat Master Jesus. We were alone on a hill. Warm breezes blew across our bodies. I could see his eyes - only his eyes - yet felt the warmth of his body next to mine. I felt his attention on me as a loved one. All thoughts of human limitation were lost to the power of only love. Our interactions were through the senses - no speaking - we were in laughter, in joy, immersed in love for each other. An energy melted into my lower spine where a caduceus tattoo resides on my physical body. This was brought alive and, while still in this envelope of love, the energy brought warmth and a feeling of ecstacy. On up through my body the gentle warmth of peace, love, well being, and familiarity came to each energy center. It flowed to the pelvis, lower back, abdomen, solar plexus, across the mid back, up into the center of my chest and on into my heart. Here it melted like warm, soft wax into my shoulders and upper back.

Onward to the throat and a sweet and gentle expansion up to the crown center and beyond, to the stars. All the love of the universe surrounded us as though we were in a cocoon of sweetness. The expansion opened and I could see around us a group of smiling Yogi's, wearing turbans. Their smiles were deep, rich, loving. No words were spoken, but we were communicating. I felt so at peace, at rest, and completely at one as I joined their circle, dressed in traditional white turban and shirt. We sat in companionship, about seven of us including Jesus, joyfully experiencing each other's company. Love and acceptance our only dialogue. I turned then, to see a most magnificent stairway which led to a throne made of jewels, rubies and light. The Being upon the throne was a vibration I recognized, though I was too lost in devotion to try to describe Her. Any descriptive words would fail to bring truth to the reality I was facing. As I approached Her I could see her loving gaze upon me, and I wept and wept as though under her spell of love. We both turned then, and looked back at what was my physical body. My hands, my face, my arms and legs. "Oh look, Mother"', I cried. "My wing is broken", and I sobbed as we looked together at the damage which had been done to my human frame. With that recognition came instant vision of all the broken winged ones who walk upon our Earth as humans, those who are feeling desire for deep connection within yet not knowing the way of repair. I saw, and heard in an instant, the breaking of the wings and the intent behind it, as something that was done as an act of violence to instill limitation and fear and compliance. The Mother recognized my understanding, and I had another moment of being overwhelmed when my pleas for humanity pierced the heavens and beyond. In one cry the ground shook, the chest spread wide open, the window for the eyes opened and I viewed eons of despair, sadness, ignorance and limitation as well as an underlying spirit of truth, possibility, renewal, hope, rejuvenation, joy. I asked then if the Mother could restore my wing. There was no answer but for the glow of light placed upon my broken, tattered wing. I and the Mother dissolved into a swirl of vibrant, violet color, my heart completely full and at peace, in love, so deeply in love, with what is now possible.

How can I possibly relate the concept of this love to my clients now? The word is so overused, but it was truly at the core of the healing energy accompanying me in the healing room. And this meditation showed me that really, there is only love - the one great principle of creation, the cohesive power of the universe. What kind of demeanor was I to adopt to convey this truth to others? We see and have experiences in our third dimensional reality, overrun with emotional and mental considerations, where bringing to the forefront the capacity of love to dissolve all discord seems unattainable. How do we penetrate these outer, self-constructed walls to get to the inner truth? How can I possibly help others find their way? Now more than ever I was able to appreciate the invisible team of Healers assigned to me. Surely they had a map. If I could just keep setting aside my own judgement so the energy could flow to others unimpeded, encourage others to stay open and allow for this flow, I would be working correctly and had a chance to influence others in profound, life altering ways.

And as with just about everything else within the healing room, it was not my design to take up the mending of wings. This idea crept into my mind subtly after I was intuitively coached to ask a client to imagine they had a pair of them. I say this out of the context of the healing room, where everything was in divine order and made sense. Here we were, working close to the body near the shoulder, and I say to the client, "I'd like you to imagine you have a pair of wings." It would not have occurred to me except that it felt exactly like the client had an open wing and we were repairing it with literal stitches when the thought came. I put this into words more easily now after some years have passed because I have grown into knowing the message is more important than the messenger.

Before I tell you more, try to imagine yourself standing in the middle of a small circle. Around that circle is another circle several inches out. Then another circle several inches out from that, and another out from that one. Each circle is filled with beautiful hues of light and they are all surrounding you. The circles continuously influence each other and move like sound waves across a vibrational field that is in motion. Now, ever so gently, raise your arms and feel with your imagination a strength attached to those arms that lifts them higher and gives them stability from a point behind your shoulders. Connected to a sense of power in the raising of your arms is the inhalation of the belly, filling and inflating, heightening the rise of the arc behind and above you. The wings are attached to the back of the heart center and across the shoulders. It may be aeons away, but the day will come when we once again walk on Earth with the attendance of visible Angels. Perhaps you will be of them.

I desired to remain in unified vibration with the Great Mother who appeared in the meditation. If I could have all of my being from my skeleton to my cells to my mind to my emotions resonating with one illuminating deity, it would be with Her. The evocative feelings arising from this intense meditation could not be sustained, but the visual image of being in Her presence will never leave me. I am She and She is Me. Before there was a He there was a She. He is contained within the She, even in our English language.

Chapter 13

"The important thing is this: to be able, at any moment, to sacrifice what we are for what we could become." - Maharishi Mahesh Yogi

My morning meditations continued to reveal deeply expansive openings within my energy centers. Simultaneously, my healing room practices were starting to feel more comfortable as I grew into understanding that the energy work done within it was emerging from a Primal Source behind the veil, and beyond my intellect. As was the case during the meditations, in my healing room I opened the door to the energy of the Great Unseen Wisdom. That Wisdom did for me and for others what we could not do for ourselves and was beyond the reach of our ordinary minds. Here is meditation number eleven, where I glimpsed the rainbow bridge and the powerful Energies abiding there.

I came to a doorway, although some might call it a vortex. My experience is that of going head first down into it and landing in a far away land with a sand floor, very bright and wondrous. The walls and floor are the same lovely color of light sand. I am escorted via magnetism again to a staircase, and again I embrace the energy of the Mother. I weep in recognition. She talks to me without words and tells me she acts as the Healer, She is the One who comes to the healing room. The energy then moves from Her to and through me, winding around my feet and moving up through my head. She becomes the ribbon and we are entwined as though the energy is a vine, stringing us gently together. The energy then connects to a rainbow, and there are beings - men - sitting on each rainbow color. Just sitting there in a pose of devotion, surrounded by light. Each one's heart is exposed to me and I resonate with their devotion to the one Great Source. There is no cause in the entire universe to make them move a muscle save for the direction of the Mother/Father energy which is Love. The Beings are stone still yet we converse without words and express our love for each other. Again, I am overcome with deep emotion and I weep. I see instantly the extent of devotion required to hold a rainbow color. There is no thought from them that is not of devotion and no cause in the universe greater than what they are now doing. I proceed to each one and stand behind them. Hues of purple, blue, yellow, orange, red, green, violet, turquoise, magenta. I circle them, pass through them, become them and integrate all they are into my consciousness. Each one a beloved friend and lover. After penetrating each one's aura, I return to the Mother and merge with her image. The bliss and ecstacy comes from a deep source within and all chakras are enlivened and changed. I am told I can return as often as I like and can bring others with me.

This meditation forever changed me. I could no longer separate myself from Divine Love. I began to feel the power of the Great Mother in my daily life and felt Her heart radiating through mine to others. This feeling has never left me. Her Love remains my constant companion, Her ribbon my lifeline.

Some days later, in my morning meditation I asked the question, "What is my medicine"?

Here is the profound virtual meditative experience that followed - meditation number twelve.

I travelled through a tunnel-like vortex. I was trying with acute awareness to look at the geometric designs composing the walls of the vessel I was traveling through. It looked like fluid with little bubbles (I have since seen this many times). I was waiting to get out to the stars, which has been a usual experience, but I went elsewhere. I was so aware of the inability to move my body, and I knew/felt a magnetic force around it which extended a foot or so away from and around my body. I had to keep reassuring myself that I was alone, door locked, because I felt like others were able to see me. My recollection that I was (in physical reality) in my living room alone was a bit distracting but did not interfere with the experience. So on and on I went, experiencing the ecstatic bliss of traveling with acute awareness in embodiment yet without restriction of the physical body. Upon leaving the vessel and getting out somewhere in ether, I heard a choir, or perhaps a quartet, singing "Mary Had A Little Lamb" and I thought at the time perhaps I was one of Mother Mary's little lambs. Additionally, I went to a beach where there were thousands of people. The sand, the sun, the warmth was wonderful. But there were too many people. I wished for a beach with no people and suddenly I was on the beach with no people. Then I wished to see my old friend Burt, and Burt appeared on the beach with me. We had a wonderful and loving conversation. On and on the experience unfolded in this manner and I found myself creating and recreating and making decisions over what manifested. My thoughts became reality. At one point I stepped into a white box and the lock sealed. I was a bit panicked because I could not get out. Inside the box there was a small shower, like in a locker room. I received a shower and the water dissolved the cubicle around me. I was free. When I was released from that confinement I walked forward, towards a wall, and stopped about one and a half feet from it. There was a Being energetically waiting for me - I do not know who - and I fell into his arms. Perhaps it was the male aspect of myself. Complete comfort, unity, buoyancy, ecstacy, bliss. An entire blending of forms into One. Indescribably delicious. The experience lasted about an hour and then I had a choice to either continue or ease out of the meditation, which I chose to do slowly.

After the meditation I knew I would act with greater intention to create and recreate my world, and that this would be my medicine. The spoken word has creative power, as do our thoughts. Energy follows thought. I witnessed this creative power over and over during the meditation as my thoughts molded one new reality after another. It affirmed what I had been learning in my studies about the power of thought. I had been working to replace undesirable thought patterns with more constructive ones such as peace, love, forgiveness, understanding. Would I now be better able to translate this learning to my ordinarily spectacular life, especially when it came to relating to family members and friends? It's a challenge we all face, even those of us with naturally optimistic natures.

Chapter 14

"If a man achieves victory over this body, who in the world can exercise power over him? He who rules himself rules over the whole world." Vinoba Bhave

Over time I had to find ways to bring myself back from these dimensions. True to form, I was experimenting on my own, and for your safety I would absolutely recommend not going it alone without a skilled teacher. But for me, I insisted on finding out for myself what the mystery was all about. At first my inner guides sent my deceased cat to intervene on my behalf to wake me up from the transcendent state. When my time to be away from my physical body was up, they would send her to gently bite my finger. I would be instantly awake. Over time, as I went farther and stayed longer, my cat stopped coming. Now it gets tricky. When my cat stopped coming, I experienced a time of extreme discomfort when I sometimes became trapped between worlds without the ability to get back. Shamans will teach you to hang on to a good strong rope before embarking on such an inner journey. But I had no such rope. I finally learned that I had to keep my wits about me, even when I was far away from this third dimension we call home, and apply what I had been learning and now taught to others. Was this the whole point of my virtual meditations? I am not sure, but once I learned how to safely bring myself back from other dimensions, the transcendent meditation experiences abruptly stopped. I got one last experience in a meditation where I climbed a tall fence, used all my strength to pull myself up to the top and took a peek over it. I saw vast blue sky, with a few clouds. And that was the end of my trips - so far. Since then I have had a handful of experiences, which have been very satisfying, but they are rare and I no longer actively seek them.

The method that finally worked to bring me back to this reality was a technique I learned and originally read about in the Ascended Master literature on "electrons." Electrons are esoterically referred to as the building blocks of the universe. Often referred to as pure spirit or light, they create order and alignment. They balance, harmonize and stabilize our many bodies, including our physical body. In the physical world they are responsible for putting the "solid" into the solidity of objects. When I was between worlds and unable to find my way back, I eventually put this teaching to work. I called on my electrons and commanded them to form my physical body. And voila', I was back. I tried it enough times to know it really worked. That says all kinds of things about the practices we adopt and why we have a practice in the first place. We talked earlier about the importance of having a practice that can be applied to life when it is really needed. Otherwise, why have a practice at all? I suspect my lesson to learn was that I had to use my "will" to command my fate. I had to take creative charge to assure my well-being, even when out in space and very far away from any human assistance. I retained my creative abilities in the ethers and that is our divine right. I just had to remember to use them. I guess that remembering was indeed my rope.

Whether on a large or small scale, each one of us is ultimately responsible for creating our personal well-being. We can lean on others when needed but it is our job, our responsibility, to take care of this divine life we have been given. The sense that I am a self contained, expansive unit with all of the grand potential and necessary power needed to exist anywhere in the Universe became my reality, my truth. This is who we are as human beings. We have everything we need within us. Dare to discover this for yourself.

Early on, after opening the business, I was drawn to place the symbol of an atom on the handouts I designed for clients. I guess I thought of it as a cool token representing life itself. I didn't realize it would be such a life saver for me down the road. Now I visualize that atomic symbol, electrons included, stamped on those early handouts and feel a strength and gratitude down to my core. Could it be that this cohesive symbol not only held me together physically but magnetically held my entire holistic practice in tender balance?

Here is the electron exercise you could find in a small book titled *Electrons*, published by the AMTF. Start with a very small health issue and work up to something more problematic. Practice makes perfect. Keep at it and don't give up.

Balancing Your Electrons

Electrons are the building blocks for restorative function. They are tiny, fluid, atomic vibrations within and around your body that are in constant motion and extremely sensitive. They are charged with obedience. In spiritual terms, electrons are pure universal light substance having intelligence within them that respond to the creative power of the spoken word. Universal light substance is yours - without limit - to mold and create as you will. As the captain of your vessel, you are the one to command the electrons with your words and directions. This is how we use our consciousness creatively to balance and harmonize our bodies. Of all the self healing techniques I've used over the years, working with electrons brings the most stability to the body. Try it for yourself. It is very simple. Lie down for a rest period of about fifteen minutes. Think of an emotional, mental or physical issue that needs healing. As soon as you lie down, speak out loud to your electrons. Here is the command you will use:

Electrons

Electrons

Electrons

Balance and stabilize my _____.

Balance and stabilize _____.

Balance and stabilize _____.

Do it now.

Do it now.

Do it now.

You will fill in the blank with your issue or problem. I like the words balance and stabilize because it brings general alignment to the body. You may choose your own words if you like. Some other choices would be release, strengthen, harmonize, align or support. You do not have to believe in this exercise for it to work on you. Try it and decide for yourself.

Part IV

Chapter 15

"It is not known precisely where angels dwell - whether in the air, the void, or the planets. It has not been God's pleasure that we should be informed of their abode."

Voltaire

My healing practice was growing and I was growing right along with it. The meditations provided a sturdy foundation for my healing room but I didn't comprehend the grounding influence of them at the time. And though I couldn't always define it, it was clear that something extraordinary was happening to my clients during our sessions. Often while on the healing table they would tell me about colors they were seeing, fragrances they were smelling, Beings of Light coming into their conscious awareness, feeling a hand on their forehead when I was standing some distance from the table, memories being released, and profound contentment arising from within. During the healing work we were continuing to concentrate more and more on opening the upper energy centers with the eye movement exercises and the placement of the physical eyes in the upward position. This technique helped bypass the mind, allowing for deeper relaxation. The breath is the only thing the mind will obey. As B.K.S. Iyengar was known to say, "breath is the king of mind." Proper breathing technique was front and center as the cornerstone for all of our healing work. It was the first thing to correct if needed.

When ready, we encouraged the client on the table to gently lift higher into the space of the crown center. This action availed a point of light above the physical body that was then drawn down into the chakra system to be used during the healing session. It was a team endeavor. The Helpers were the inspiring teachers, I was the communicator, and the client made the effort. We could assist, but no one else could do it for them. When the client lifted the belly with inhalation while simultaneously lifting the ocular muscles of the closed eyes upward, as in the exercise mentioned earlier, they gained beneficial access to the Light of self expansion. It freed them from being so tangled up in their mental and emotional problems and gave space for the release of built-up tensions. My reality told me they were also opening to a connection that emanated as a tube of Light above the physical body. I routinely reached up into it to retrieve or magnetically draw down a strand of that Light to attach to one of the chakras.

As an energy healer I now realized I was in the position of being an etheric mediator - one who stood between the worlds. As was discussed earlier, the client's etheric body, almost always invisible to the naked eye but palpable to those of us who are tactile practitioners, acted as the bridge to higher realms. During a healing session, it was particularly useful for me to be in touch with that aspect of their human nature because it was the area where pure energy, the energy of Love, resided. It was energy untouched by human thought or emotion. And though it would try, even the mind could not fully penetrate that sacred realm of etheric energy. So, when applied judiciously, as it was during our healing work together, the true nature of that Love had the ability to dissolve areas within the mental, emotional, and physical bodies where injury, fear, hurt, etc. had been trapped. Because of the existence of this Love, such disturbances simply fell away. This allowed the injury to be released and simultaneously infused with new life force which had the potential to heal old wounds.

I thought I loved deeply after all my years of living, raising children, being married, and developing long lasting friendships. But my earthly love felt somehow superficial compared to the endless love emanating from the circle of Helpers appearing in the healing room. Sincerely, there are no descriptive words to explain the expansive opening created in the heart while in Their presence. My heart took on a life of its own, relinquishing all ties to my earth bound life as it rushed to merge with the one Soul focused in our group.

Though I received healing rays simply by being in proximity to the Helpers, They did not come to the healing room to see me. They specifically manifested dimensionally to bestow their healing skills upon others for the good of humanity. When the session was complete, we all went on with our day. But lucky for me, it was evident that during the meditative state, I was granted the gift of physical perceptibility through the senses of touching, smelling, seeing, hearing and tasting. It was so superbly satisfying to ascend high enough to briefly coexist in the atmosphere with the Angels, Masters, and Healers, and to have a glimpse of Their physical presence never revealed in our healing room. Those experiences helped me immensely and erected a solid, impermeable inner connection that I rely on to this day. It also reassured me that I was indeed interacting within an expanded realm of existence that included the healing abilities of great Teachers and Masters who seemed to have the aptness to blend into my form to minister to others through a pair of human hands and a devoted human heart.

While it was wonderful to have the client lying on the table for an hour or more, in reality, I had gained enough proficiency that the energy work could now be done in much less time. Also, it was clear to me that I had been permanently changed in that I realized I was now surrounded by wonderful Attendants continually, not just while in the healing room. This may have always been the case, as is likely true with all of us, but up to that point I'd not had the awareness of such Presence. It was not disconcerting, but felt quite natural to be in this expanded awareness. If I put my attention on Them, there They were. If I carried on in my life as though They did not exist, no problem. The choice was entirely up to me. This was quite a realization and fostered a deeper relationship between us as my exchange of energy with Them became more creative. I started experimenting with the energies as ideas came to me on how to use them in my daily life. I wouldn't want to reveal all my trade secrets, but for example, I would choose one or more of Them to send ahead to prepare a space we were about to enter, or to stay behind and offer a blessing to someone who had requested help, or tend to someone who was ill, or offer a kindness to one who was in need. We operated on a shoestring of Love. I would send them out to help others knowing that at some point they would circle around and return to me all the better for being of service.

For the purpose of demonstration, you can do the same with your own team of Healers. Use your imagination. In your mind, imagine an entire row of little angel beings sitting on a bench before a game waiting for their turn to play. They have been practicing and perfecting

Their skills for a very long time. You are the coach, wanting Them to succeed. You have tremendous faith in your team of players and you know They are ready. You trust Them to do Their job in the field and you want to see Them try. The "game" in this case is the same game of life that you are currently involved in. And the "field" is the place you are living in right now; your home or your office, your neighborhood, your city, your country. The little angel bench warmers around you have been preparing for a very long time to assist you and have been waiting for the go ahead. Nothing can be done without your say so. Give it a playful try. Use your words to send one or more of Them on a mission to be of service to another. Notice the joy it brings to you, knowing those little beings, your Helpers, are shining Their very own radiant light to another on your behalf. It's enough to melt your beating heart. As childishly simplistic as this exercise sounds, it is actually a basic technique meant to help you practice your skills as divine creator.

After all these discoveries, practices, experiments, and experiences, I could finally let down my guard enough to relax into my new truth. Not just in the healing room, but in my life. I wanted to be the same person outside of the healing room that I was inside of it. I wanted to have the same kind of life outside of the healing room that I experienced inside of it. I wanted to retain the same seamless connection at all times that I felt while doing the healing work in my circle of Helpers. If I could assist on any level of existence, I was completely willing to do so. I didn't know exactly what it meant to be a healer but I had immeasurable desire to be of service and was devoted to my Soul who had made it attainable. It felt impossible to now close up the healing room at the end of the day and take up another persona outside of that room. Not only would it have required enormous energy to do so, but it would have been cutting myself off from the vital source of life that now supported my very being. I was living in this reality that included limitless access to Help. The Help was available in a heart beat, any time day or night. Slowly I embraced the enormity of what had been happening through my meditations and in my healing room. The combined effect created in me a turning point and once again, there was no going back. I asked to have the courage to maintain equilibrium and remain centered while I consciously let go yet again of the she I used to be.

Chapter 16

"One thing: you have to walk, and create the way by your walking; you will not find a ready-made path. It is not so cheap, to reach the ultimate realization of truth. You will have to create the path by walking yourself; the path is not ready-made, lying there and waiting for you. It is just like the sky: the birds fly, but they don't leave any footprints. You cannot follow them; there are no footprints left behind." Osho

I prepared myself to witness enhanced spiritual experiences now commonly seen with the clients who came through our doors. The

Helpers met them at their evolutionary threshold and did their utmost to gently lift them a bit higher. Some future affairs are written in the stars, and no matter our action, destiny will likely occur. Yet, often times one needs to be nudged in the right direction. One aspect of my role was to encourage, offer support, and infuse faith in the client's ability to move into a possible scenario that hovered just beyond that threshold. Like the outline of an undeveloped photograph, the client's future was poised to materialize based on a continuum in space and time given the client's current desires and abilities. The Helpers often eased them through these transitions during our sessions. If a fear surfaced and had to be energetically removed, or the invocation of an affirmation needed to be decreed to move past an obstacle, we did so.

There seemed to be an underlying motive of evolutionary momentum surrounding the methods we employed to hasten the arrival of the client's future into the now. The attitude of the Helpers was an expectant and quiet confidence that all of us, including me, were absolutely capable of moving forward. Their confidence made it impossible to shy away from accompanying them into Their Light. They were showing us the way and my clients and I willingly followed. For anyone who has ever entered our healing room, I can tell you that even though we may not be close in proximity, we are still supported and connected within that structure of Light.

Everything seemed doable while in session, including helping clients move into their future. But it was one thing for them to step into their future while in the safety of our healing room, and quite another for them to apply new ideas and ways of being while out in the world of their homes and communities. I struggled mightily to appease collective worries and doubts, and I handled many late night phone calls asking for spiritual reinforcement from my clients. I was able to do this work with ease while in the healing room, but I was not prepared to have an entire fleet of clients step into the unknown at the same time, juggling their fears and dreams, looking to find sure-footedness within the four walls of our healing room and looking to me to help them navigate the waters of change. I did my very best to reassure my lovely clients and gave encouragement, but, oh lord, a sense of being overwhelmed threatened my personality, and had it not been for my overactive sense of responsibility I may have run for the hills. The growth spurt required to develop a comfort zone around this issue surely added to my head of gray hair. But in the end it was worth it. I overextended myself repeatedly until finally getting relief by remembering that it wasn't all up to me.

The appearance of the crystal, my transition into holistic health, the existence of the Helpers, the influence of the Masters, the meditation experiences and the clients who received illuminated Light were all timed perfectly to pull us through an evolutionary worm hole. Our clients were absolutely capable of holding Light and sat at the forefront of evolutionary change. Each one was equipped with everything they needed to move forward. The lessons I learned during that time of intense responsibility have remained with me to this day. Although at first I suffered when my clients suffered, worried when they worried, and became afraid when they were afraid, I found a way to release those limiting emotions by sharing them with the greater forces available in the form of the Helpers. Like reflecting a wound to the sun, I reflected our client's burdens toward the Light of our healing circle. A burden shared is a burden healed. We were all in it together. It is true that this form of prayer helped to release my own fears and worries. But a greater truth revealed the availability of Divine Intervention for the client reflected back to them in the rays of hope, joy, love, compassion, and stewardship from higher realms. It is an Angel's job to radiate. It is our job to ask. It is safe to say these divine forms were well employed during those first years in the healing room. Their radiant qualities formed the womb of transformation for so many of our clients who were in the midst of life changes.

Masters likewise poured their healing balm onto our clients, though likely holding the tarp of protective Light over them leaving just enough exposure to the storm for the client to make a correction, if needed. The Master energy helped the clients grow into the form that was waiting for them, and learn the valuable life lessons so needed to move into the future, all the while blessing that client with the very essence of the Master themselves. Today I can see that we safely made it. Things fell into place and the energies held within the crystal were given the freedom to express once again in the world of form and matter. Humans, Angels and Masters worked dynamically together, expressing through our healing room and beyond.

Chapter 17

"Hence, there is a time to go ahead and a time to stay behind. There is a time to breathe easy and a time to breathe hard. There is a time to be vigorous and a time to be gentle. There is a time to gather and a time to release. Can you see things as they are and let them be all on their own"? Lau Tze

By now my healing practice had been open almost a year and my office lease was ending. I had yet to realize the profound influence my meditation practices had on my healing room activities because I was still trying to keep up with my new role in life as a healer. Thankfully my meditations had constructed a strong and resilient connection of love and compassion that held a steady rhythm for me during my day to day interactions and supported the work that continued in my healing room. Outer worries still infiltrated my peaceful, meditative mind from time to time, but I was gaining ground and confidence and was starting to feel more qualified in the world of holism.

My husband and I had an offer to become the live-in caretakers of a healing arts building soon to be completed in Madison, so I planned to relocate my healing room to that setting. A beautiful new healing room awaited me in a beautiful new building with windows and abundant sunshine. I was thrilled and excited about the move and had a lot of enthusiasm. When the time came to move, the transition from one healing room location to another went smoothly. Once we became the caretakers, my healing room continued to thrive, but I gradually stopped the intensity of my meditation routine. Two things happened that contributed to this ending.

First, I became very busy with the role of caretaker of the new building. The work and the people there became vitally important to me. I did not allow myself the privacy or the time required to sustain the intensity of the meditations. While the traveling experiences during them were a breathtaking side effect, I did not have control over whether the meditations did or did not happen. When they stopped occurring naturally, I felt I'd gone just about as far as I could go at that point in my seeking. Perhaps it was rationalization, but I sensed the assimilation of energies needed to sustain healing room activities had been completed for now. I became filled up with Light, just like the clients who came to see us, and I had absorbed to my capacity for the time being. A pattern seemed to be emerging now over and over in the healing room regarding beginnings and endings. Like filling your car's gas tank to the brim, we filled a person up with as much Light as possible during a healing session. Rearranging and rebalancing, birthing new energies, releasing worn out patterns, radiating Light, Light, Light, as much as could be handled at one time, and exposing one's energy body to the Masters, Angels and Others who attended healing sessions. The impact of such changes could not be reliably weighed and measured.

We then sent the client out into the world attached in new ways to invisible threads of Light that would help induce positive changes for them over time. The time for those changes to occur depended on many unknown factors, and we couldn't exactly predict with accuracy how soon to expect them. Most changes happened very subtly, but they would eventually materialize, even years later.

As a result of the outpouring of Light, it became clear in my mind that I would have to temper the amount given over time to individuals. It's not that there is a short supply of Light in the universe. There is not. But we are able to absorb only so much at one time to assure complete grounding and assimilation for the effort put forth. So we would not want a client to come back to the healing room too soon after receiving a potent energy infusion, to give them enough time for assimilation. Likewise, the same rule applied to my healing room in general. We eventually had to stop every so often, with regularity, and wait for some unseen evolutionary wave to catch up to us. I had the very distinct impression that the Helpers were keenly aware of timing, and we could proceed only so fast. I had to discern these stops and starts, which often coincided with seasonal changes, and I trained myself for the difficult task of erecting boundaries with my clients regarding when I could see them. This was an unpleasant undertaking because, as I said, I was inherently a people pleaser and it took strenuously applied effort to change my pattern by learning the art of saying "no."

Second, it was simply time to let the meditation practices go. This was not easy. I didn't suddenly decide one day to drop them, it happened gradually. Or maybe the practices decided to drop me! I tried to hang on to them, but it became a struggle and I no longer had the desire to persevere. Anyone will tell you, it's hard to keep up with something when your heart is not in it. Should I have pushed through and insisted? Maybe. Highly trained practitioners will tell you to keep up the practice especially when you feel like quitting. And that is generally good advice. I could have gone that route. But I did not choose to. I felt like I had to make a choice to move forward into the life that was now being presented to me, or stay back and wait for the next thing to emerge.

I kept up with my yoga asanas, and continue to do them to this day. And even though it was my choice to release them, the loss of the meditation practices left me feeling bereft. I could see how they had been a stepping stone for me and an incredible tool for transformation leading me to the very position I now held. Had I gained enough sustenance from them to hold the vibration now needed in this new role? Had I learned how to embody the energies of the Christ Consciousness to allow the radiation of that energy to influence others, and to anchor through my very being that sacred energy in and around my surroundings? I did not realize during my time of ardent studies and practices that I was being prepared to do exactly that. The transition of letting go of the daily meditation practice felt like a slow walk across an unsteady bridge that could give way at any moment. Could I keep my eyes straight ahead and not look down? In this role as caretaker, I was in the position to apply, on a broader scale, the skills I had learned in the healing room. It became clear to me that we could use the work in the healing room as a pattern, an overlay, that could be applied to limitless settings, particularly the one I was now in. If I had the availability of unlimited Helpers, and They had access to expanded Consciousness then together we could create without limitation.

This staggeringly complex realization would have been incomprehensible to me prior to this year, but now it rang true with exquisite simplicity. Of course. Creating is our birthright. My meditations taught me that space and time have no constraints. The size of things was of no concern. I was involved on many other planes of existence with my conscious mind while lying on the couch in my living room. Elegant life forms came to share these experiences with me as represented by Jesus, Master Healers, Angels, Teachers, the Yogis and the Great Mother. Colors and other healing rays demonstrated my connection to a rainbow of light. I had exquisitely skilled Helpers in my healing room standing next to me in service to others for the good of us all. Could I dare take the lead and direct this life force toward an idea that I now invented? Had my heart grown pure enough to put my creative birthright to use and try a new idea on a greater scale? After all, the healing room was the perfect space for "trying on" new ideas. What if we placed the healing arts center on our healing table and proceeded as though it was the focus of our healing instead of a client? Hadn't this been what my meditations had been preparing me to do? In my mind, I was being invited to test our collective skills by expanding the borders of our healing capacities to include this new healing arts building and all the practitioners within it. I had been charged as the caretaker and felt a responsibility to help others when they asked.

I can see in hindsight that at the point of letting go of my meditation practices, a coinciding shift occurred in the healing room. My personal meditation practice came to an end, but it was the beginning of an expansion with the Helpers. Even though I had reached the edge of the boundaries in my meditations, the boundaries in the healing room collapsed, exposing infinite possibilities.

Chapter 18

"A star falls from the sky and into your hands. Then it seeps through your veins and swims inside your blood and becomes every part of you. And then you have to put it back into the sky. And it's the most painful thing that you will ever have to do and that you've ever done. But what's yours is yours. Whether it's up in the sky or here in your hands." C. JoyBell C.

My new office space evoked a different kind of energy than my prior one, plus I now had the fine company of dozens of other skilled holistic practitioners all under the same roof. On the second floor of the building, my office felt more open and cozy. I placed the crystal in the sunny window and she responded by reflecting her gloriousness on all the walls and even on people while they rested on the healing table. I considered placing her in the foyer of the building, as had been suggested. Frankly, I did not trust that she would be safe there, as so many people came and went through the front door. At least she was above the foyer and in that way she continued to radiate to those entering the building. It still emitted the heavenly scent, though I noticed the fragrance as much outside as inside of the healing room. I had been studying ascended master literature over the past couple of years, and brought some of those teachings into the new space as well. Their names and qualities adorned my windows, colorfully written in crayon. I'd not thought it out at the time, but I see in hindsight that the reflections of the master's names and their qualities co-mingled with the reflective light rays of the crystal and brought to fruition the prophesy written about in the email. Indeed, here the crystal and master energies worked together with the help of the bright southwest sun to diffuse, project, and indelibly imprint their sacred union onto the walls of our new healing space.

I'd like to proudly say I chose those ascended master teachings all by myself because they seemed comprehensive and inclusive to all races, genders, and religions. But the truth is, I had anonymously received a book about them in the mail while still employed at the University two years prior. So it was not my idea to seek counsel through that literature. Again, the universe had intervened on my behalf. The material found its way to me. The book arrived shortly after acquiring the crystal and here again was reference to the masters. When the book came into my possession I devoured it immediately, such was my resonance with the information. It made sense to me. I felt a connection to the teachings then, and that relationship has remained strong all these many years later. It's really the only body of work that helped me sort out and then define the energetic healing activities taking place in my healing room. They helped me feel more comfortable in my skin. I guess that's why they grew on me with such favor that I've learned as much as possible over the years since then.

The influence of those teachings sustained me during the first couple of years as I transitioned into my role as a holistic practitioner. Undoubtedly, they also contributed to turning our sails toward the horizon of change that surprisingly began to surface after the move. No sooner had we arrived in our new office space when those changing dynamics began to appear. And just when I was getting comfortable with the status quo! The cessation of my meditation practice brought a palpable change to my healing room, exposing to me a glimpse of endless potential. I felt empowered and ready to work. The entire healing space was now rearranged not only to include a new room and building but also the master energies, leaving an opening that felt as wide as the sky.

Yet, as exhilarating as that feeling was, underneath it I felt a groundswell of growing unease emanating from deep within me, and I noticed in my bones the tiniest rumble of an earthquake. You know the feeling of a premonition? That unmistakable knowing within that tells you something is about to happen, but in spite of yourself you try to carry on as though you did not hear the faint whisper of that secret? I didn't know why, but the dark realization came to me then that I would be closing my healing room. I didn't know when, but I *knew* it was going to happen. There it was, in front of me, as clear as if someone had written it on a piece of paper. I cannot describe to you the depth of grief I felt when that thought struck me as truth. It literally took my breath away. Devastation seared my heart. Would I be able to bear the loss? My mind zoomed to the future and imagined a lifeless, empty void without the joyful presence of my Helpers, and I was seized with panic.

As quickly as it came, the feeling dissolved from my mind, and in came a parade of Angels, smiling, moving past me one by one, just as they had done in my meditation. There were no words, but there was understanding. I could hear a message coming from Their collective intention, which told me to relax and carry on. Nothing was amiss. All was well. Life is dynamic, changing, evolving. Life flows. The sun rises and the sun sets.

Reassurance was immediate when I had a stunning realization that brought a clear perspective for me. In the meditation, the Angels were not the ones moving at all. I was the one who was moving and had been doing so all along. I couldn't have stopped even if I'd wanted to. What was that telling me about my own evolutionary path? I was still learning and always would be. Was the healing room really a stepping stone and not a stopping point? That had definitely not been my plan. And here I was, caretaker of a healing arts building, and that hadn't been in my plan either. Life was carrying me along, offering options, and I suddenly glimpsed with great clarity the timelines that lay ahead. If there was a benevolent divine director engineering on my behalf, tracking a life patterned after the stars, I yearned to cooperate with it. In fact, I swooned at the thought of aligning with such a force.

There was now a lot to consider. I'd had the good fortune of recently sitting in audience with Domo Geshe Rinpoche, a wonderful and precious flesh teacher of mine at the time, who'd smiled and said to me "don't let any grass grow under your feet." I thought it an odd comment and hadn't paid much attention. I could see now what she meant by that statement. What others might later perceive as unpredictability, I would learn to honor as timing.

My healing room had lots of starts and stops before it finally closed for good. And I should not have been surprised by that eventual outcome. The feminine energy of kundalini is constantly fluid and in motion. She is the great mover. I felt a renewed kinship then, to this dynamic energy which was the foundation to my healing room. I was grateful to feel its presence. But at that moment, when I realized the healing room was an evolving, living, breathing entity that was also likely on a timeline, I was going to make the absolute most of it while I could. I recommitted to the moment, hid the destiny of my healing room on the back burner of tomorrow and jumped into "now" with both feet. I would worry about my exodus from the healing room when the time came. What I didn't realize then was that the Helpers had already been permanently woven into my being and we moved as one unit regardless of our location. We were inseparable and integrated. Even though I had been actively practicing with them outside of the healing room, I hadn't yet developed enough trust that they wouldn't abandon me without the healing room as home base.

Chapter 19

"Life is a series of natural and spontaneous changes.
Don't resist them; that only creates sorrow. Let reality
be reality. Let things flow naturally forward in whatever
way they like." Lao Tze

I had to find a way to balance all of my new responsibilities inside as
well as outside of the healing room. The situation at hand revealed
involvement and work in the new healing arts center, and there were
only so many hours in the day. It was no longer a simple issue to carve
out certain times when I could see clients. At no other point in my life
was I more comfortable and in unity with my soul than while being a

caretaker to this lovely three story building and her people. It became my holy dharma to be of service in this way. The building itself became my healing room, and provided a container big enough to hold all of the Sacred Energies emanating from my healing practice.

So I realized early on in this caretaker role that it would be too much to continue a busy private practice and still manage my other responsibilities. The idea of working with groups came to mind as a natural and evolving next step in which to apply our skills. Doing so could potentially offer wise and conservative use of our collective energy. Group work had been surfacing within my healing room since the move to the new building, but I hadn't yet worked out the details of how to proceed. Did I know what I was doing? I had no experience with group healing but I had been reading about the many benefits of such activity. It seemed clear that group work would allow us to move evolving souls together rather than individually. Energy works efficiently in a group. It has a deeper, broader impact on the world and planet when it is radiated cooperatively through group consciousness. The premise of group healing work for me would be to harness the skills and healing techniques I had learned in my healing room and reflect them on a broader scale.

While the idea of group work stayed with me, my personality had to sort through the logistics of transitioning from individual sessions to group work. I really had to slog through my people pleasing instincts and I had a hard time letting go of disappointing clients. Especially in light of my recent "knowing" about my future in the healing room. Here I had all these Helpers available as a gift for others and I had the nerve to say to people I would not see them in the healing room? In hindsight, it's more true to say it's not that the dynamics of our healing room were changing when I felt the premonitions. The shift had already happened, but I hadn't recognized it. It took me quite a while to unify with that reality. I viscerally understood the next phase for me was to take a step back and practice working with the "many" instead of the "one", and part of me wanted to soar ahead and leave everything behind in the dust. But a thousand pounds of responsibility held me back. Way back. That's a nurse for you. And, oh lord, I loathed telling my clients I couldn't see them for individual sessions. It just felt wrong. As a nurse, I inherently related to people one on one. My clients did not want to stop individual sessions, and I completely understood why. There is nothing like sitting with another and carefully listening to their story to set the stage for the restoration of good health. In my healing room, this availed the client to have deep and personal conversations with me and allowed for questions and time for reflection. During our sessions, as the client on the table expressed themselves in whatever way was most useful, I was able to listen and then assist with a multilevel healing process. Attentive listening is what we all do on a daily basis to help other people - our family members, our friends, and others who present themselves to us each and every day. The fact that I had a healing room and Helpers to assist perhaps gave me more credibility as a healing influence, but believe me when I say we are all capable as healers and we should never think otherwise. To help with the healing process is to be available to another in a kind and compassionate way. I offered a space away from the grind of every day living and housed the Helpers who benevolently extended their radiance to bless and uplift those in need. And yes, we worked to collectively enrich the evolving nature of each one who came in to the healing room. Yet we all have healing abilities at our fingertips.

I had learned over the past year how to lift my hands off an individual's physical body to work in the expansive and invisible field of their energy body. I hadn't been entirely sure of the existence of an energy body only two years ago, but here we were, putting all our eggs in that veiled basket. Thankfully my doubts about that had completely vanished. This healing practice had become all about energy. It was clear to me that the space within the invisible energy field held incredible potential, and the images that had started coming into my mind revealed to me the direction we were now heading. If we could apply energy to one, we could apply it to many. It seemed a path was being created, not just for me, but for our devoted sphere of Helpers and the work we were doing together. As the proprietor, I could choose whether or not to go down that path. Had this been the plan all along?

Was this the natural flow of order and an expected leap into the next phase of our development, or was I making the whole thing up for some bizarre and hidden reason which I might coyly be keeping from myself?

The thought of making a mistake under the pressure of my healing room responsibilities worried me. Once more, this is where my insecurities came into play. I wanted to do the right thing. I had not anticipated such a change in our healing style.

Unsure about how to proceed, I sat alone in the darkness of my new healing room one evening, quietly searching for a clue to help me understand and asking for clarity around the premonitions I'd been feeling about shifting from individual to group work. In those days, after the meditation experiences ended, I'd sometimes receive a clear picture in my mind to help me see where I was headed. I had learned to relax into this technique, as it was now the form of communication that worked to relay information from one realm to another. After sitting there for awhile, in my mind's eye a brilliant core of vibrating Light appeared. The vibration held steady and then the radiance from this great Light began to spread, gently impressing a steady outward balance of luminescent calm. I couldn't discern if the Light was pushing away the obstacles, or swallowing them up but ultimately the Light grew and the obstacles faded. Stationed within those Light waves, those resonating, gentle, powerfully unstoppable waves of Light, were the Helpers from our healing room. And in that moment of recognition, the wings of our healing room lifted a bit higher as the Helpers and I sat together in the stunning, joyful image of this expanded vision, feeling the camaraderie of our individual positions in the shared Light of our shared destiny, experiencing our shared devotion to the work, to each other, and to the Light itself. No borders existed to contain that Light, and nestled in between the Helpers were circles of people. I could see there were limitless Ethereal Beings tending to each person in every circle grounding them in the Light itself. As long as this window was held open, the humans in the circles received such illuminated attention. I knew then the path of group work was the correct one to take. "Go forth and multiply", as the famous quote implies. I would say today that if you are reading these words and you have been in one of our healing circles, take a moment to pause. You are receiving radiant and healing light through the connecting lines of our eternal Love.

For a short time I tried to do both, individual and group work. It seemed quite do-able in the beginning but as time moved on, the individual sessions started to wear on me. I didn't see then that a line had been drawn in the sand when we took on the new paradigm of focused group work, and the part of me that had indeed soared ahead was waiting for the rest of me to catch up. Today, I fully realize I was stationed at a point in the Light, and as long as I remained there, I was comfortable. But when I strayed back into what "was", as in doing the work I did in the beginning of my practice, my body complained. I was being invited to keep moving forward. It seemed so true, the phrase "don't look back" became my new mantra. When I tried to contain the energy, as during an individual session, I started to feel a restless and impatient urge tugging at my conscience, telling me the one at a time work was too slow. And my body started complaining with physical symptoms that I now had to manage.

Personally, I hadn't yet developed a skill set to take our work to a group setting but I absolutely trusted the process and knew it would unfold in perfect alignment. I was ready to diversify and move forward. After all, the Helpers themselves were a group.

Of course, a group working with a group made perfect sense. I am all for acceleration, so I took the chance and started offering group healing workshops and group healing sessions. We then proceeded to do the same kind of healing on the many as we did on the one. Once again, it was amazing to be in the midst of this possibility.

When we started the group healing work I could hardly believe the strength of it. So, so many Helpers appeared to assist others. I was expecting a handful of folks at our first group offering. Imagine my surprise when over 40 people arrived. Ethereal Helpers tended to each one, as though each participant was an individual client in our healing room. So many Teachers, Masters, Healers, Angels, all under that now familiar Umbrella. There was one great source of Light with countless emanations, all colors of the rainbow, all inclusive and focusing on individual needs within our mortal circle. The speed by which we could work together was impressive. I must admit, it was infinitely easier than individual sessions. My body handled it better. I could do the work without having conversation, and it took much less effort to direct the energy without having to explain the dynamics while doing so. When my clients came in understanding they were receiving the same healing in a group as in an individual session, they were able to relax and receive. Additionally, words are not necessarily appropriate after a healing session and it's best to keep the mind passive during that time. It's certainly good to have understanding, but first we should give permission for the new energy to settle in, and it will inform the mind over time. This helps one connect on inner levels and keeps the healing between the self and the Self. Nothing external can penetrate that inner core which will sustain you through all the storms of your life. It is both an anchor and a life preserver.

The best scenario, from my perspective, is to lie down, surrender to the energy, allow Spirit to do the work, breathe in, and release whatever needs to be released. Then be in silence. This is where the interlocking connection happens. It is not with me or with the Helpers. It is with the Self, and the more we can do to make that happen the better off we all will be. I tried to stay out of the way and not interfere with this connection during healing sessions and in group work. But in our culture we are used to asking a lot of questions and applying our logic to figure things out. In general, people gave way too much credit to me for bringing about a shift in perspective for them. Even the Helpers will step aside so one can know their greater Self. Everyone in-between those two points, the Masters, Healers, and Guides, whether in human form or not, are all stepping stones. And when others start to lean too much upon one of those stepping stones, that stone will likely withdraw itself lest it become a premature stopping point. Such is the power of Love.

If it was infinitely more satisfying for a client to come to the healing room for a one-on-one session than a group healing, I will never know because they never complained. I love my clients for making that offering.

I understand it's not true for everyone, but I have to admit I like change. And I like a challenge. I also like doing something just to prove to myself that it can be done. I could see other practitioners in our building and around the city who seemed so stable in their practices and did not change anything in their healing rooms. Most practitioners would have been thrilled to have a busy practice such as mine, and I wished I could be like them. But I couldn't. In fact when the certainty of group work became more defined, the part of me who soared ahead felt relief wash over her like wild fire. She couldn't wait to break out of the confines of what had been created.

Perhaps it is rationalization, but I believe it was the destiny of the healing room to expand in this way- the way of the group. Adjusting my personality to the dynamic healing room changes took more time than I like to admit, but all considered, we have weathered those changes. We have now expanded to include an even wider swath, encompassing many levels of healing on a planetary and even cosmic scale. We are stretched to the limit, in a good way. Those expanding circles of light emanating from the one great Light continue to spread outward, influencing, swallowing up, and harmonizing obstacles and dis-ease in our world today. The Invisible Wisdom Keepers, Healers, Masters, and Angels are all stable within those circles of Light. Like the constellations, They are in Their assigned place at all hours of the day and night, ready to be of service.

Conclusion

Chapter 20

"What the caterpillar calls the end, the rest of the world calls a butterfly." Lao Tze

It took many years before I permanently closed our healing room, but we have not stopped offering our healing work to the world. While we are now working on a broader scale, and I am standing at a distance, our radiance is no less fierce. In fact it carries more punch than ever. We sustain a global presence in our world today. Now that some time has passed and I can reflect, I see that the healing room was a paradigm for our Earth itself. We are living and existing in a healing room if only we take the time to consider and realize it. We have the availability of endless Healing Companions as close as our heartbeat to assist us when needed. The Source is within and all we have to do is ask. If one of us can do it, any one of us can do it. Not only that, the radiance is there. It is just a matter of allowing it to shine. As Thomas Merton said, "Life is simple: we are living in a world that is absolutely transparent and the divine is shining through it all the time. This is not just a nice story or a fable, it is true".

My healing room became the container for trying on new ideas and ways of being in our world. We created a restful time away from the outer world where clients could reflect on their spiritual growth and life changes, while their Helpers radiated dynamic, evolutionary healing energy to them. This energy exposed a longed for feeling of Divine Presence in the client, thereby stimulating the cooperative effort between them. It was magical. Intoxicating. A slice of Heaven on Earth. The Helpers made it so. It seemed to happen so quickly, the realization that I had become the healing room. I realized my Self as complete.

When I first closed my healing room, I worried the Helpers would abandon me. Funny how I attributed human qualities to Their divine natures. It took a long time to realize we are inseparable, forever and eternally, and we are woven together like the fabric in a beautiful cloth. Today I also realize that you and I are inseparable. We are One. I strive to treat you with love and respect, and I know that as I do so I also treat myself with love and respect. When I speak to you I am also speaking to myself. As has been said, the body never forgets and that includes the words we speak and the thoughts we think. I need to take care that I honor myself by honoring you. If I can keep that practice up I will exist in a healthier body with a more peaceful, open mind.

Of course, there is ultimately no limited boundary for Universal Energy to express itself. It was entirely my made up notion in reference to the possibility of containing such energy, as though it could be structured and held together by a barrier of any kind. My personality could only move ahead so fast with the evolutionary changes that transpired over the course of a few short years. My small self had to construct boundaries so I could safety integrate the largesse of what had been exposed to me. I am aware that each one of us has the capacity for such an expanded nature. How much of it is made available for our use is really up to us. Spirit will give us as much as we desire. I have always liked to control my circumstances, so the Energy kindly worked around my quirks. Circumstances manifested when it was time for me to test new waters, and I was continually invited to move beyond my comfort zone. In that regard, my clients were not the only ones asked to do so. We experienced a communal evolutionary growth spurt. Whether they knew it or not, I was with them every step of the way. The Helpers and I now stand in our positions, holding a location in space and time, knowing that no matter what threatening storms approach we will hold steady in the Light. As amazing as it was to be working in the healing room, how fulfilling is it now to provide for others the stability of the healing rooms' fully opened wings.

Throughout my story, I frequently used the terms "energy" and "Light". In this context, energy is the spiritual force running through all things. It is a broad term that became the common thread tying together my healing practice, the Helpers and my acquired style of healing. Light is nature's way of transferring energy through space and is a form of Consciousness that connects everything in the universe. It explains itself. It can be felt with your whole being by attuning to unconditional love. When you feel this energy, it radiates, affecting those around you positively. In our healing room, Light helped awaken dormant energy within. The Helpers appeared as a reflection from a source of Light beyond our physical reality. Sometimes the Light in our healing room was so bright I had to don a pair of sunglasses.

I also chose to capitalize references to my Helpers, and I did so as a means of expressing my devotion and gratitude to Them. I just couldn't help myself to do otherwise.

My experience has taught me that I do not exist alone. And I believe you don't either. There are blessed ethereal Beings of Light who work in impersonal service and assist with our process of living. Some call them Masters and Guides, some call them Angels, and of course they are all of those. They are the loving, compassionate "Spiritual Tools" in our energy bodies. They know where we are going and where we have been. They assist with integration and help organize the unity between our various bodies. These Helpers are not visible to most people. But like the wind that blows the leaves on the trees, they are very real and influential. I remain deeply connected to the realm of ascended masters, and their energy remains present at all healing activities. Masters in the truest sense of the word, they serve as world Teachers from the realms of spirit and can help us grow in any area of our lives. We were an evolutionary team and often pushed our clients to the edges of their comfort zones. We were stretching the margins of reality to include new possibilities, and if the clients had not been ready they never would have appeared in our healing room.

Here's what I like to imagine. That each one of us came from the heart of Source with an indwelling Light tucked deep inside the Self that was activated long before we appeared on our beloved Earth. This Light remains vibrationally unsullied, grounding and reflecting to us our true nature - the nature of Love - so that we can ultimately identify and remember ourselves through human form as interconnected cosmic beings who share the same unified, divine heartbeat. The remembering of this Love Light connection carries the solution to the confusion and dysfunction in our world today.

I believe the Helpers appeared in my healing room to guide us back home to the Light of our very own unique and wondrous Self. Within the Self lies the potential for one's personal life path. Some might call this a divine plan. There is enormous power in knowing what is true specifically for you in regards to that plan, and claiming it whether it is popular or approved of by others. As your divine plan unfolds it may not look like anyone else's. It carries the stamp of individuality because you are one of a kind!

So, this is where my story ends. The boundaries of our healing room dissolved, and it became impossible to contain. We outgrew our four-walled Healing Paradise, and expanded out into the world and beyond.

The crystal remains active and the Masters will determine her fate. She continues as a vehicle for Their energies, which enliven and empower human consciousness for the good of humanity. Together we became a beacon of Light, and a reflection of the Divine. I am the first to say I was the lucky one who showed up and became a willing device for these reflective rays. That is all I can take credit for. Somewhere in my past is a vague memory of commitment when I uttered the words "I do" and signed on the dotted line. In that way there was a marriage of sorts between us, and perhaps a prearranged contract that was determined eons ago to be honored at a particular moment in time and space. Such is the power of destiny. It's not what I have or have not done that will matter to me in the end. Of course, being a loving, kind, compassionate, and helpful person is what I strive for. But most satisfying for me is the sense that I fulfilled an obligation, come hell or high water, and there was plenty of both. I have done what I came here to do. Nothing trumps that feeling, though grandchildren are a close second. I am complete.

And so we say goodbye for now. To those of you who've been in our healing room, we look forward to seeing you again. To those of you who've not yet arrived, we look forward to meeting you. The healing room will open her doors again; it's just a matter of time.

Epilogue

I have extensively studied Ascended Master literature. There is a lot of it available, and I've sifted through much of it. I was drawn to the writing not only because of the book that arrived anonymously in the mail at the beginning of my holistic health career, but also because of the letter from the woman who talked about my working with the "Masters" via the crystal. Although I was not familiar with the Masters when I received the crystal, I assumed they were a body of Enlightened Teachers who helped humanity achieve the same. I claim to be no expert on the matter. However, since the very beginning of my journey, when the teachings first came to me, I was drawn to them like a moth to the flame. I understood the writing on a very deep level and committed my entire being to be of service in whatever way I could. I loved the idea that there could be an entire group of Enlightened Beings of all colors, genders, races, and religions shepherding the human race in impersonal service to help awaken them and bring about a renewed sense and obligation to the true Self.

This book essentially wrote itself as an explanation for the series of healings brought to humankind through the combined efforts of myself and my Helpers. It now belongs to you. This writing allowed me to truthfully tell my story. It is now yours to do with as you will. You may use the meditations as your own, and I hope you will do so. We offer many blessings to you as you continue on your spiritual journey.

Steps For Manifesting Your Ideas

Have your "will" to do. Truly, what is it you want? State it clearly.

How are you going to do it? What is your plan? State it clearly.

Love the endeavor. Is this your heart's desire? If so, express it with deep feeling.

Clarify your original design. Use your imagination to picture it.

Affirm and concentrate on your idea.

Repeatedly give your idea the power of your intention.

Surround your idea with peace. Envelope it with tranquility.

Creative thinking patterns

In its essence, energy itself is unformed. It must have a thought form, a receptacle, some definite pattern which will receive it and enable it to express the divine design for which it was intended. The "vision" the mind pictures is the pattern into which the life essence will flow. Energy follows thought. Without a definite pattern or a vision of higher things, of something better than the present manifestation, the energy keeps getting denser as its vibration lowers into habitual thinking patterns. So I encourage you to "look up" by practicing a meditative technique or resting your eyes at your brow.

To look up is to see hope. In this way, you are the creator of your life force. Work to avoid the return of heavy, unwanted energy of fear, anger, resentment, doubt. Train your mind to be peaceful and tranquil and concentrate on those qualities to magnetize and hold the lighter vibrations within you. You might use a mantra such as "I AM Creator", "I AM Light", or one of my favorites, "I Stand In The Light Of My Own Perfection". If you slip back into negative thinking patterns, take a moment to lift your eyes to the center of your brow or forehead, inhale through your belly, and ask for help which will come from your perfected Self. You do not have to name the Help and you do not have to believe in it. But you do have to be willing to ask. Never underestimate the power of your will.

Mantra

I recommend you find a catchword, or a phrase, often called a mantra, that resonates with you to use as a touchstone for centering yourself when you start to veer off course. The power of a mantra has been acknowledged since time began. A mantra can consist of a powerful word, or group of words, and is used to bring you success, peace and contentment, self-actualization, release from worries, or to fulfill your heart's desire. The range is extensive and you can choose one for yourself.

I use mine endlessly from dawn to dusk and to help with sleep. A mantra will vibrate to your core and resonate within you to assure unity on all levels - emotional, mental, spiritual and physical.

For starters, you could choose the vowels in the English language, A E I O U, which are perfect examples of healing sounds. Repeat them over and over to yourself. Often a spiritual teacher will give a student a mantra and in that case, the word, or words, are charged with the mastery behind the teacher's teachers. But you don't need to have a teacher give you one in order to use a mantra. Find one that feels right to you, and then commit to using it. Over time, your mantra will provide a safe harbor and peaceful retreat from the rigors and stressors of daily living and open you to knowing your Self on deeper levels.

Printed in the United States
By Bookmasters